TO. AL

30 J

CL.

LIP IT

MACHINE IT

DELIVER IT

SELL IT

GET PAID FOR IT!

HAVE A GREAT & WELL

DESERVED HOLIDAY.

NEIL.

DIG IT
BURN IT
SELL IT!

The Story of Ibstock Johnsen
1825 - 1990

BY MICHAEL CASSELL

A Pencorp Book
in the Pencorp Management Series

Published by:
Pencorp Books.,
Beagle House,
80 Hill Top,
London NW11 6EE.
Tel: 01-458 9343.
Fax: 01-455 7828.

ISBN No: 1 870092 01 5

Set in 11pt Bookman and printed by Biddles Ltd., Walnut Tree House, Woodbridge Park, Guildford, Surrey GU1 1DA.

Photo reproductions by Rory Isserow.
Current board photograph by Gerry Rushton Ltd.
Design by Peter Greenwood of The Production House.

CONTENTS

ACKNOWLEDGEMENTS

THE story of Ibstock Johnsen has been a fascinating one to write and the job of delving back over more than a century and a half was made easier by the willing co-operation of a large number of people.

The book was commissioned by a company that is, of necessity, pre-occupied with the present and the future but which, fortunately, decided to record the past before it slipped from view and from memory. The time taken out by so many to help me in my task is greatly appreciated, as is the independence which has been extended to me throughout.

Members of the board have been especially helpful in my efforts to assess the group's strengths and weaknesses, its triumphs and failures. Paul Hyde-Thomson, in particular, whose knowledge of brick and of Ibstock is unparalled, has been an ever-obliging source of information and reminiscences.

I must extend my thanks to past members of the board who have helped build up the Ibstock story. Those who may have had a less high-profile role in the development of the business have proved equally supportive and my special thanks go to the company pensioners who contributed their own special memories of a business for which they retain a deep affection.

I must single out Roger List as the principal link between the group and the author. Ready to help in the search for information right up until the eleventh hour, Roger has always given me his characteristically courteous support which has been invaluable.

I must also thank Paul Hannon, my researcher, who has travelled more miles than I in fitting together the pieces of the jigsaw and who has tracked down some of the more elusive subjects required for interview.

And my thanks, as always, to Arnold Kransdorff, my editor and publisher, who has let me get on with the job but who has always been on hand when I needed him.

Clunton,
Shropshire.
January 1990.

PREFACE

MEN have made bricks for six thousand years. It was only in the 15th Century that the word "brick" came into common usage in Britain; before that, the blocks of clay used for building were called "waltyles." Set in that historical context, Ibstock Johnsen is a rank newcomer to the world of brick.

The feet that trod the clay and the sun that baked the crude finished product in Egypt and Babylonia have long since been replaced by more reliable and efficient systems of production. But while the process of brickmaking may today be shrouded in computerised technology it has, essentially, changed very little over the centuries.

The business, which began life as a coal mine in Leicestershire more than 160 years ago and now produces one billion bricks a year, has played a central role in again making fashionable a once-neglected building material. Its success in helping to provide a new dimension to the world of construction by offering a quality alternative to the run-of-the-mill brick has not been founded on anything as straightforward as technical excellence. Ibstock Johnsen has always seen brick in a different light.

While the product might be just another commodity, the business has succeeded in promoting it as something much more special; it has won its profits by convincing others of its case. Where some saw uniformity and commonality, Ibstock envisaged attractive variations, pleasing profiles and endless tones and textures. It has been a company of vision and a pioneer of building tastes which has enabled it to carve out and command a niche in a highly competitive market place. The story of Ibstock Johnsen is one of Victorian determination and contemporary ingenuity and skills. The debate about whether brickmaking is a science or an art, or an intriguing combination of both, is never-ending but no-one can doubt that the company whose history is unfolded here has made its mark in countless buildings on endless streets. It has stamped its name on generations of building development.

To most people, a brick is a brick is a brick. They know little about how they are made and care less for those who supply them. They are a product so commonplace that, in isolation, they provoke little comment and even less passion. But as an attractive, versatile yet practical building component they can, when part of a whole, create pleasure and inspiration.

Ibstock's mission has been to ensure that those responsible for building a nation's fabric shared its love of brick and an enthusiasm for its ever-widening application in the face of fierce competition from other building materials such as concrete and wood.

After years of unspectacular but solid progress, the business finally blossomed after the Second World War in the hands of the fifth member of the same family.

Ibstock began to build for itself, by a process of acquisition and expansion, a range of bricks and a growing national reputation as a manufacturer and supplier which did not believe its contribution to the world of construction ended with an order.

It has survived as an independent force in an industry now controlled by conglomerates, its own characteristics as distinct as some of the bricks it produces. Ibstock has always remained close to its customers, helping to shape demand as well as to respond to it; it has led more often than it has followed.

Ibstock customers can expect advice and assistance on a scale which extends well beyond the remit of a brick manufacturer, an approach which has served the business well and which has nearly always enabled it to ride through downturns with a style which has made it the envy of some of its competitors.

There have been bad times, however, and there have been moments at which the future of the business looked extremely bleak. On more than one occasion it could have been consumed by bigger businesses anxious to claim such a valuable prize.

Though seen as a company operating at the leading edge of the brick business, it is still sometimes regarded from outside as a conservative operator. The view cannot be entirely justified, given its ambitious moves into Europe and into the United States, both of which at one time appeared to have been bad mistakes.

It is, however, still thought of as a family business. No such description can fit a publicly-quoted company whose ownership lies in the hands of numerous institutions and individuals. But there is a style about Ibstock, imprinted upon it by its own history, which helps perpetrate the impression. It is not an unhelpful image, conveying a picture of gentlemanly expertise and experience, of concern for its employees and its customers. In every other respect, Ibstock is a very modern operator.

Whatever its history, the group must look to its future. It has achieved its ambition to become a national supplier of facing bricks in the UK and must decide how else to broaden its base in its domestic market.

Overseas, where it sells twice as many bricks as at home, similar strategic decisions have to be taken. Europe, the scene of its most famous past failures, also awaits as moves towards economic and monetary union draw the community ever closer together.

They are challenges which Ibstock must confront. If its future bears any resemblance to its past, it will meet them and turn them to its advantage. It will build a future as sure and sound as if it were made of brick.

Mr Robert Hyde Hyde-Thomson, blinded in the Great War but nevertheless a principal architect of Ibstock's success, which was shared and inspired by several generations of the same family. Born with the christian names of Robert Hyde, he subsequently assumed the surname of Hyde-Thomson when his father decided to incorporate his own wife's maiden name into the family name.

I

In search of buried treasure

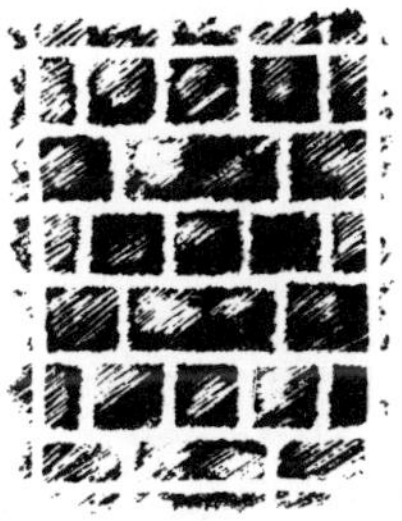

IN 1825, as Mr. William Thirlby, a farmer and lacemaker of Ibstock Lodge in the County of Leicester, sank a crude pit-shaft to search for coal, a rapidly-industrialising Britain was enjoying the novel experience of an economic boom.

Mr. Thirlby, like countless other businessmen, was starting to enjoy the fruits of a buoyant economy and was sufficiently encouraged by his personal sense of well-being to seek further wealth beneath his own fields at Ibstock, a few miles to the north west of Leicester. Prospects appeared promising after some tough and traumatic times.

The Napoleonic Wars, finally brought to an end only a decade earlier, had left an agricultural and industrial depression in their wake along with a wave of social unrest and organised protest which had been stirred up by high unemployment and low wages.

The agitation which had stemmed from the distress of the "working classes," a term which had only recently come into use, helped sow the seeds of socialism and the first stirrings of unionism.

There were numerous popular uprisings which gave the 15-year-long administration of Lord Liverpool cause for continuing concern and which led it uneasily from oppression to reform. In 1816, at the end of a public meeting at Spa Fields in central London, an angry mob had set off towards the City to riot and loot. It was dispersed with some violence and the incident provoked considerable alarm at Westminster.

There was growing unrest far beyond the capital. The following year a hunger march set out from Manchester to demand the reform of an unrepresentative Parliament and the scrapping of repressive legislation. The so-called "blanketeers," a motley group of blanket-carrying handloom weavers, were easily dispersed by troops and got no further than Derby.

The same year saw a pathetic attempt by unemployed textile workers in Nottingham to march on the city demanding provisional Government. For their troubles, 14 were transported and four were hanged.

In 1819 a mass meeting of workers from all over south Lancashire met at St. Peter's Fields in Manchester to listen to speeches on the need for political reform. Despite precautions to ensure there was no violence the local cavalry were called in to restore order, leaving 11 people dead and 400 seriously injured.

Within months a conspiracy to blow up the entire cabinet and seize London was uncovered. One Arthur Thistlewood, its principal architect, took his place in the history books as the last person in England to be beheaded.

The source of such deep-seated discontent was easy to locate. Although agriculture remained the biggest single occupation, growing numbers of people were now working in industry, many of them in mechanised workshops and factories.

For many, an average working day lasted for anything up to 12 hours and working conditions generally were wretched. The most dangerous work of all was probably that of the miner.

Down the pit men had to accept explosions, flooding and roof collapses as ordinary hazards. The chief miners, the "undergoers," lay on their sides, clearing away coal to a height of little more than two feet with their picks. Boys were employed to clear away the coal loosened by the men.

In some pits women were also hard at work, carrying baskets of coal or dragging trucks. One woman of 37 described her conditions: "I have a belt round my waist and a chain passing between my legs. I go on my hands and feet. The pit is very wet where I work and the water comes over our clog tops always. I have seen it up to my thighs; it rains in at the roof terribly; my clothes are wet through almost all day long."

Regularly the team would be crushed or buried alive in tons of cascading coal. Miners would fall down shafts, get struck by collapsing timbers, fall from the ropes or skips which took them to the surface or were crushed against walls by passing coal trucks. If they were lucky, they would work until they were about 40, unable to go on because of lung disease or ruptures.

Children were used as trappers, opening and shutting trap doors intended to control the circulation of air in the mines. As in other industries, they were often beaten. Cruelty was rife.

Women and girls played a major role in other industries, not least in the manufacture of bricks. They made them on moulding tables while girl assistants, or "pages," brought them the clay and carried off the finished bricks for firing.

The women would often be employed on the basis of producing a fixed number of bricks a day. It was hard work, carrying heavy loads of six or more bricks at a time. With no restrictions on the age of children employed, some of the girls were only six or seven when they started.

In the coalfields which straddled the Derbyshire-Leicestershire borders people had been earning a meagre living for centuries. Some workings dated back to Roman times and one of the earliest recorded coal-bearing areas in the district was at Swannington, just to the north of the new pit being opened at Ibstock.

As far back as the early 13th Century coal mining was well underway in the area. Similar operations were to spring up throughout the district over the next few centuries at places like nearby Coleorton, Measham, Newbold and Heather.

Many pits were small and short-lived but, by the start of the 19th Century, names like Donisthorpe, Oakthorpe, Packington and Lount had been added to the local coal mining community.

The workings were as numerous as the small granite quarries which littered the countryside and which also were left derelict and potentially dangerous. The sudden disappearance of at least one grazing cow down a newly-gaping chasm is on the record to demonstrate one of the many hazards which the mines left in their wake.

By the early 1800s some of the mining operations were taking on a grander scale. The Earl of Moira took a lease on 3,000 acres of land on the Ashby Wolds and, by 1805, his men reached coal at 1,000ft. A nearby canal gave the operation a ready-made transportation system and the mine prospered.

The year before William Thirlby's coal shaft was sunk at Ibstock, on land his father had owned since 1777, mining had started five miles further north at Whitwick. Other pits in the locality were to follow in quick succession, at places like Bagworth, Snibston, Gresley Wood and Swadlincote.

In the year of Ibstock's birth another development to the north, which would have a profound and permament impact on the nation's industrial life, was taking place. Though railways were not new, they were not regarded as a suitable form of transport for people. In 1825, however, the first public steam railway was opened between Stockton and Darlington in County Durham.

With considerable ceremony the first train was preceded by a man on horseback, carrying a flag, and driven by Mr. George Stephenson, the railway pioneer and builder of the wrought iron route. The engine was called "Locomotion" and the long line of wagons behind it, weighing 90 tons, eventually reached a speed of 15 miles an hour.

Other lines and many more engines would quickly follow.

Stephenson, who was also a colliery owner, foresaw the ultimate impact of his own endeavours. Drinking with friends one night he told them: "I venture to tell you that I think you will see the day when railways will supersede almost all other methods of conveyance in this country - when mail coaches will go by railway and railroads will become the great highways for the King and all his subjects."

By 1829 the Ibstock colliery was tapping a rich seam of coal lying at various depths on a site which stretched to well over 100 acres. But although it had steadily built up its market for coal among those local businesses utilising steam-driven machinery, Thirlby had run into financial problems caused by the sizeable borrowings he had arranged in order to finance the development of his pit.

He had initially raised £2,800, half by mortgage with a Mr. Joseph Jephcott of Exhall, Coventry, and the balance in the shape of loans bearing 4.5 per cent interest and raised against his house and land. He had, however, under-estimated the capital required by the business and raised his mortgage, as well as borrowing a further £350 from the Rev. Thomas Storer of Great Wigston, near Leicester. Even this proved insufficient and he was forced to seek partners in return for fresh funds.

Even so, the losses continued to pile up and, by 1831, William Thirlby was declared bankrupt. His share of the business and his farm at Ibstock were seized by the Rev. Storer and he died a broken man a few months later.

After a protracted legal wrangle between the remaining partners, James and Benjamin Cort, the Leicester ironfounders, ownership passed to the Rev. Storer's two sons, who decided to invest more money in the colliery, notably in deepening the shafts to reach a coal seam up to 8ft. 6in. thick.

By now the second railway line in England had been built along the 30-mile route between Liverpool and Manchester. When it was opened there was just one locomotive in use, the remainder of the railway's traffic drawn by horses attached to the front of the crude carriages. Even the locomotive had a horse and rider in front, with passengers often perched on top of the coal.

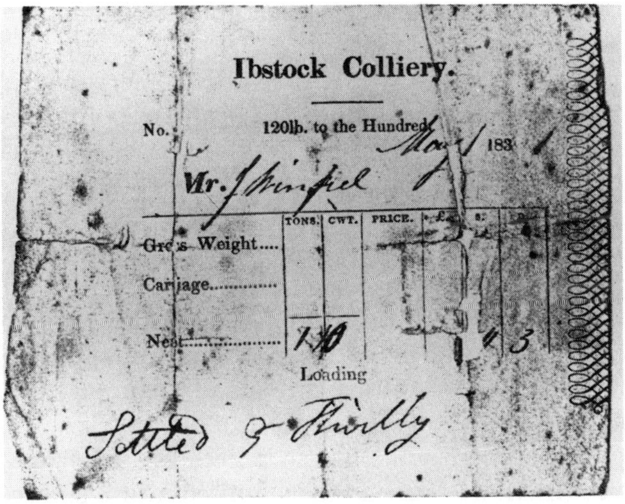
Ibstock Colliery.
No. 120lb. to the Hundred 183
Mr.
TONS. CWT. PRICE. £ s. d.
Gross Weight....
Carriage............
Nett..............
Loading

A colliery weighbridge ticket, dated 1831 and signed by William Thirlby, the first man to mine coal at Ibstock.

While the route was being built George Stephenson had won a competition for the best design of a steam locomotive with an engine he christened "The Rocket." The splendidly liveried machine had a top speed of 29 miles an hour and was capable of pulling behind it a load of 14 tons; its continuing existence provides a romantic testimony to its creators original genius. As "The Rocket" was making its public debut, so Robert Stephenson, the son of its inventor, was busy surveying and laying out the nation's third major rail route between Leicester and Swannington. The line was also intended to provide a rail link to several nearby collieries, most notably the pit at Whitwick which was owned by Mr. William Stenson, who had befriended the Stephensons.

While Robert grappled with the challenges of driving his railway line north west from Leicester, the Leicester and Swannington Railway Company was approached by the new owners of the Ibstock colliery and asked to consider the construction of a branch line to run from what was to become known as Ibstock junction - 11 miles from Leicester at Bagworth - to the pit. The new link was added to the blueprint.

The line was to cost an estimated £75,400 and the newly-created railway company raised share capital of £90,000 and a further £20,000 by mortgage before work began. Powers to enable the project to go ahead were enshrined in the Leicester and Swannington Railway Act of May 29, 1830.

The Ibstock colliery owners agreed with the railway company to foot their full share of the bill and, two years later, the one-and-three-quarter mile, single-track line, constructed to a gauge of 4ft. 8½in., was ready for use.

Running across lands for which the colliery owners agreed to pay rent, the branch line ran from a point near Bagworth "within a farm in the occupation of Thomas Whitehurst and extending to or near to the coal mines now opened in the parish of Ibstock."

In early July 1832 the Leicester-Swannington line opened. George Stephenson himself drove the first train comprising a passenger coach and a number of coal wagons, one of which housed a band playing suitably stirring music as the procession advanced. In another, a small cannon fired celebratory shots at intervals along the route.

Passengers clutched solid brass tickets issued from a room in a hotel which was temporarily rented until suitable premises were eventually provided. A sand-glass was used to govern the intervals at which trains could pass through a tunnel on the route and, at nights, a lighted candle in a station window would indicate if the driver was expected to stop.

There would be early, inevitable mishaps, one of which led directly to the invention of a safety device which became synonymous with the age of steam railways. After a local farmer had escaped with his life from an argument with a train Stephenson asked a musical instrument maker in Leicester to design a "steam trumpet" to be worked off an engine's boiler. The experiment was successful and the steam whistle was born.

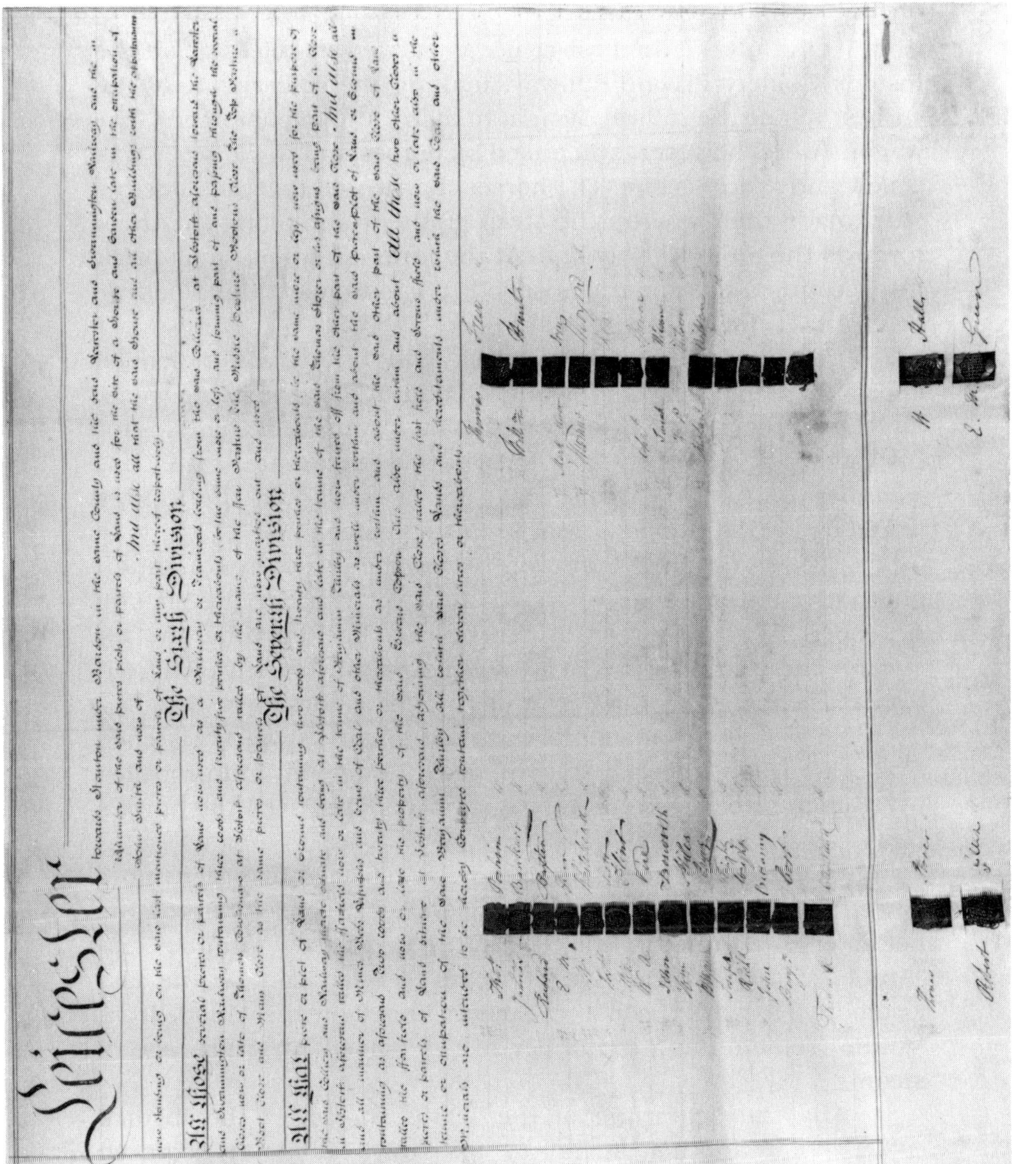

A conveyance, dated 1839, involving the sale of assets at Ibstock and bearing the fading signatures of some of the first people to be linked to the business.

On July 17 the first coal was carried to Leicester on the Ibstock Colliery Private Railway, making the colliery one of the earliest to use the railway system to distribute to customers. The wagons were, however, still pulled by horses and the journey was a slow and arduous one. The horses, harnessed together side-by-side, made their way up the steep gradient and along the track towards the main railway line. At the junction was a small brick hut, occupied by a man whose job it was to allow the plodding consignment of coal on its way.

The arrival of the rail link had immediate beneficial effects for the colliery, "affording, in addition to the home trade, a ready market with a priority in distance over other collieries for disposing of the excellent coal at a moderate rate, but remunerating price." In its first year of operation, the railway would carry 5,400 tons of coal from the Ibstock pit.

It was not long, however, before the company sought an alternative to the horses upon which its distribution system still depended. Within a year of the branch line opening the pit owners had commissioned a locomotive engine of their own from Robert Stephenson's Newcastle-upon-Tyne workshops.

The hissing machine was, not surprisingly, christened "Ibstock." Huge wheels, cast five feet in diameter and propelled by 16-inch stroke, steam-powered cylinders replaced the horse's hoof.

The engine would eventually be replaced by other, more powerful workhorses, like "Samson," purchased from the Leicester-Swannington line, the "Little Red Loco," "Jumbo" and "Annie," which would give 60 years' service and be the last locomotive to work the Ibstock colliery line. Only the whistle from "Annie" remains as a reminder of the golden, if grimy, age of steam.

By the beginning of the 1830s, however, the Ibstock colliery had another string to its bow. The land acquired primarily for the extraction of coal, which was mainly of inferior quality, was also yielding useful supplies of fire clay and clay capable of producing a high-quality brick. Workings like those at Ibstock would sow the seeds of a future non-fletton brick industry on a scale which its pioneers would never have imagined.

Brick production had almost certainly not been in the minds of the owners, particularly since bricks had not enjoyed much popularity as a building material in the early part of the 19th Century.

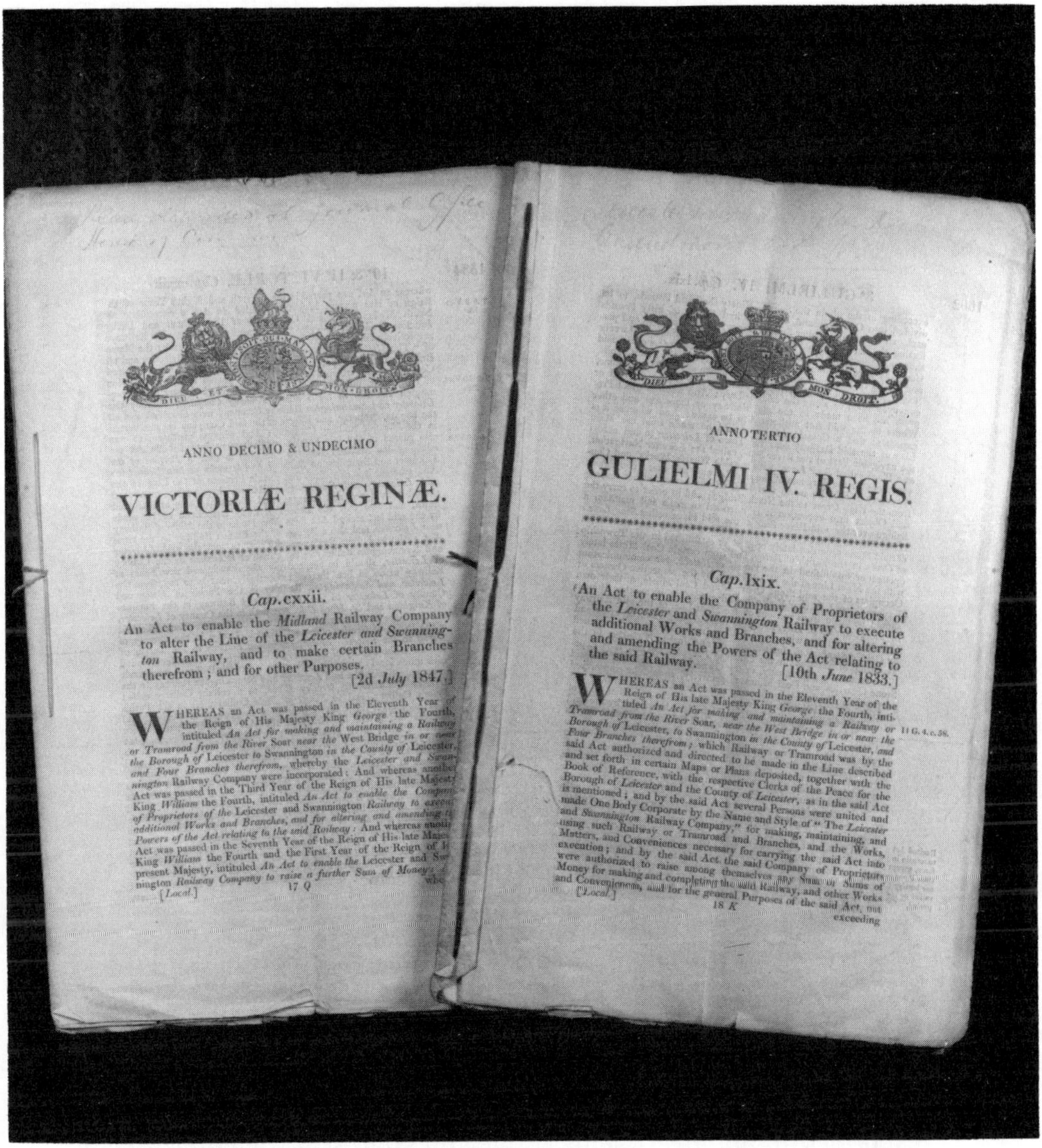

Building the railroad: Two of the enabling Acts dated 1847 and 1833 which paved the way for the Ibstock colliery branch line.

Forty five years earlier a tax had first been imposed on bricks and then subsequently increased. Even more decisively, there was now a strong predeliction, which had spread downwards socially, for hiding all brickwork behind a coating of stucco. Brick, it was widely felt, gave a poverty-stricken image.

The result was that, although brick remained a comparatively cheap building material, was easy to handle and offered speedy construction, it was widely frowned upon.

Given the scale of the Ibstock operation and a weak market production was extremely limited and remained a by-product of the main business, with apparently little scope for growth.

There was, nevertheless, some investment made in the brick operation to the extent that, by the mid-1840s, the Ibstock site also included a brick yard and a rudimentary kiln. Clay holes were opened up and worked, with teams of ponies drawing the tubs of clay to the brick shed. The poorest coal found its way straight to the brick kiln.

The impending arrival of mechanisation in place of the old hand processes, however, was about to bring a renaissance to brick. No longer would it be necessary to expose the clay to the weather; the drying could be done by machinery. Moulding, too, could be done by machinery rather than by hand, while the invention of the Hoffman kiln in 1858 meant that the fires would no longer burn intermittently but could stay alight continuously, day and night.

In 1846 the Ibstock colliery operation - "partially opened about 20 years but only in full work for about 10 years" - came up for auction. It had changed hands 10 years earlier when the Storer family sold out to the Leicestershire Coal Company, a joint stock company formed by a group of investors who had responded to an advertisement offering shares in the enterprise at £25 each.

It represented a new form of colliery ownership designed to spread risk in a risky business. Among the 28 shareholders, most of whom were tradesmen and merchants from the Leicester area, were Benjamin Payne, a local auctioneer, Thomas Pochin of Normanton Hall and William Miles, a Leicester coachmaker. Mr. Edward Mortimer Green of Ashby acted as the company solicitor.

By the mid-1840s, however, they wanted to sell out, their

Ibstock, Leicestershire.

VALUABLE COLLIERY AND FREEHOLD ESTATE.

TO BE

SOLD BY AUCTION,

BY

B. PAYNE,

(Subject to such Conditions of Sale as will be then produced),

ON THURSDAY, THE 2ND DAY OF APRIL, 1846,

At the Queen's Head Hotel, adjoining the Railway Station, Birmingham,

AT TWO O'CLOCK,

ALL THAT VALUABLE COLLIERY, IN FULL WORKING, CALLED

THE IBSTOCK COLLIERY,

Including an excellent Pumping Engine, with Cylinder of 64 inches diameter, three Boilers, and 156 yards of Pump Trees, Clack-doors, Rods and Iron Work complete. Also, a Winding Engine, Cylinder of 24 inches diameter, six feet stroke, pumping and winding apparatus, and two Boilers. Also a small Winding Engine, of 18 inches cylinder, and 5 feet 8 inches stroke, not in work, together with two well conducted Shafts and Flat Ropes, Capstan and Rope, with other Machinery on Pit Banks, Weighing Machine, Railways, and other effects connected therewith.

AND ALSO,

98 ACRES OF EXCELLENT ARABLE, MEADOW, AND PASTURE LAND,

In fine condition, with a FARM HOUSE in the centre, Barns, Stables, Sheds, and all the Customary Buildings, in complete repair, situate at Ibstock aforesaid, contiguous to, and now occupied in conjunction with the above Colliery.

The Colliery has been partially opened about twenty years, but has only been in full work about ten years.

The Estate contains several Seams or Beds of excellent Coal, the principal of which, so far as has yet been ascertained, are as follows:—The five feet or top seam, extending under 58 acres, of which about 32 acres have been worked out, and the eight feet or bottom seam, under 116 acres, of which about 23 acres have been exhausted.

There is an abundance of Fire Clay, which may be turned to great advantage, and a good supply of Brick Clay, with a Brick-yard, Kiln, large Shed, &c. for its manufacture, now in full work.

A Branch Railway of about a mile and a half in length belongs to the Colliery Estate, and connects the same with the Leicester and Swannington Railway, at a distance of about eleven miles from Leicester, thus affording in addition to the home trade, a ready market with a priority in distance over other Collieries for disposing of the excellent coal at a moderate rate, but remunerating price.

There are various Cottages and other Buildings and Conveniences on the Estate, not only for the occupation of the Farm, but also for Colliery purposes, including New Offices and Storeroom, capital Blacksmiths' and Carpenters' Shops.

The Estate is Tithe-free, with the exception of about forty acres, which pay a modus of £1. 7s. 6d. a year.

The neighbourhood of Ibstock is thickly populated, and wealthy, and the extensions of the Midland Railways, now in contemplation, will afford a new and very large market for the coal towards Rugby and Northampton, and other places in addition to the present trade in the neighbourhood, and to the town of Leicester.

The Coal is particularly adapted for the working of Steam Engines, as it possesses great powers of generating steam.

To view the Colliery and Estate, apply on the Premises, and for further particulars application must be made to Mr. Green, Solicitor, Ashby-de-la-Zouch; or to the Auctioneer, Mr. B. Payne, Market-street, Leicester; (at whose Offices Plans of the Estate and Colliery workings may be seen), and to Messrs. Austen and Hobson, Solicitors, 4, Raymond Buildings, Gray's Inn, London.

The London and Manchester Direct Railway is projected to pass within about two hundred yards of the Colliery.

ALSO, TO BE SOLD AT THE SAME TIME AND PLACE,

A FIFTY-INCH CYLINDER,

Recently bored, with Cylinder top and bottom, Piston and Piston Rod, two Cross Bars and Iron Plate 4ft. 10in. by 4ft. 11in. one-and-a-half inch thick; 46 feet Steam Pipe, 12-inch bore, Match-boxes, Clack Door-piece, Nozzle Pipe, &c. 78 feet Pump Trees, 15-inch bore, 108 feet ditto, 8-inch bore, with windbore, working barrel, &c.

ALSO,

A number of RAILWAY COAL WAGGONS, together with the Stock of Timber, Iron, Colliery Rails, Mining Utensils, and other effects belonging to the Ibstock Coal Company.

ALSO,

The Company's Tenant-right to a spacious WHARF, at Leicester, capable of conducting a very large trade in Coal, Lime, Timber, and other articles.

Ashby-de-la-Zouch, March 2nd, 1846.

The Ibstock estate - embracing farmland, a colliery and ample reserves of fire clay - go under the auctioneer's hammer in April 1846 at the Queen's Head Hotel, Birmingham.

decision no doubt encouraged by a recent fresh outbreak of social unrest which led to mass meetings throughout the Leicestershire coalfield and to the threat of riots, prevented only by the timely intervention of the Leicestershire Yeomanry.

Ibstock's owners decided upon an auction sale with a view to achieving the highest price for the business. Potential purchasers attending the sale at the Queen's Head hotel in Birmingham on April 2 were being offered "several seams or beds of excellent coal." Although 55 acres had already been worked out, nearly 120 acres remained to be mined. In addition to the railway there were "various cottages and other buildings and conveniences on the estate" and blacksmiths' and carpenters' shops.

The auctioneers described the neighbourhood of Ibstock as "thickly populated, and wealthy." They also referred to the proposed extensions of the local railway network - the London and Manchester line was projected to pass within 200 yards of the colliery - which would "afford a new and very large market for coal" in the region and well beyond. The coal, it was emphasised, had "great powers of generating steam" and was therefore particularly well adapted for the working of steam engines.

The sale proceeded and, although the identity of the immediate purchaser was not recorded, Edward Green, the solicitor to the Leicestershire Coal Company, shortly afterwards emerged as the owner.

Ibstock's performance remained modest during the early part of the second half of the 19th Century, a period which brought mid-Victorian prosperity for many and which saw Britain rightfully dubbed the "workshop of the world."

In 1855 the pit raised just under 20,000 tons of coal and, by using stocks, sold nearly 22,000 tons. Large coal was priced at between 8s 4d and 9s 2d a ton. Around 90 per cent of sales went by rail, well over half to customers in Leicester and the remainder as far afield as Leamington, Aylesbury and Northampton. The business also manufactured 469 tons of bricks.

There was a lull in social reform during the period dominated by Lord Palmerston - not to be rekindled until the emergence of Gladstone and then Disraeli - although there were undoubtedly some improvements in working conditions. Even so, the damaging labour disputes which had hit the coal industry continued and Ibstock's coal reserves were declining.

In 1866, one year after the death of Palmerston, Edward Green sold the colliery to Mr. William Whetstone, the wealthy and influential co-owner of Whitwick Collieries. He did not, however, repeat the successes he had achieved elsewhere and, by 1873, as a Factory Act which limited working hours for women and children was going through Parliament, he and Thomas Tertius Paget, his partner, arranged a sale to another group of businessmen. The deal was to mark the start of a family connection with the Ibstock company which would flourish for more than a century.

At the same time as the sale the Midlands Mining Wages Board was being set up to fix and adjust wages periodically. Mines inspectors were appointed to help encourage and, if necessary, force the pit owners to improve conditions for their employees.

The same year, however, saw the beginning of what was termed "the great depression," when British manufacturers began to pay - not for the last time - for their failure to innovate in a period of rapid change and increasing foreign competition. Company profits were hit badly and unemployment began rising again. The Ibstock Colliery Company did not escape unscathed.

The new owners' concern at the health of the colliery was adequately reflected in the minutes of their first shareholders' meeting on August 31, 1874, at the Cannon Street Hotel in London. The business owed its bankers around £800, a position which the partners resolved to improve by launching "a sorte upon our many debtors." Neither was there sufficient working capital to spend on equipment at the mine which was "very much worn out and exhausted."

To add to the company's problems demand for coal - now selling at around 18s a ton - was poor and daily production was hovering around 350 tons a day compared with a maximum of 500 tons achieved in better times. Inevitably the miners' wages were cut and they were under pressure to take still lower wages.

Mr. George Wilkinson, the chairman, intoned: "We are suffering from paying our pitmen very much more than they ought to have. We are entitled to a deduction of at least 20 to 30 per cent in the rate of wages. Up to the present time, we have only been able to get 10 per cent."

He told his colleagues that the company's neighbouring competitors were in the process of winning further wage cuts and that, under an agreement with the men, Ibstock would be able to reduce its own wages by the same amount.

The pitmen would not have been best pleased if they had heard the remaining part of the chairman's remarks. He pointed out that, though the accounts looked distinctly unhealthy, the board proposed to pay a dividend. It was, despite the fact that the company appeared to be "suffering from such poverty," a question of policy to do so.

The move was resisted by one of the shareholders, Dr. Samuel Thomson, who was from Motherwell - the town of which he was to become Provost - and who already ran a large and successful coal mining operation at Wishaw, close to Glasgow. His small stake in Ibstock, which was far from being a large or prosperous business, did not prevent him from making repeated suggestions on how to change the company's fortunes. Dr. Thomson had already caused something of a fuss by suggesting the company should prepare and circulate to directors and to the 78 shareholders a set of monthly accounts so that the company's progress could be closely monitored.

He reported that the system was already in operation and working well in his Scottish colliery and asked: "If it is good enough for Scotland, why should it not be good enough across the border?" The only objection, Dr. Thomson suggested, could be on the grounds of expense and that would amount only to a few shillings. Despite some directors' protestations on behalf of Mr. Robert Bland, the already hard-pressed company secretary, Dr. Thomson's idea was accepted.

When it came to the question of the payment of a dividend Dr. Thomson believed that, as there was no cash in hand, there should be no distribution of funds. There were angry exchanges with the directors, who eventually got their way. But Dr. Thomson's spirited arguments on a range of issues prompted one shareholder to nominate him as a director.

The move was rejected as unconstitutional given that no notice of the proposal had been provided. Dr. Thomson - "a man of great experience in collieries," according to his proposer - nevertheless offered whatever assistance he could to the company.

Mr. Wilkinson, having presided over a meeting which must have been considerably more lively than he had imagined, said the matter would be given consideration. He stressed that Dr. Thomson was not known to the company but there was no doubt he was "a very practical man" who could most likely

IBSTOCK COLLIERY COMPANY, LIMITED.

BALANCE SHEET,

June 30th, 1875.

Dr.

	£	s.	d.	£	s.	d.
TO CAPITAL.						
4,524 Shares of £5 each fully paid	22,620	0	0			
9,333 „ „ £2 10s. paid	23,332	10	0			
	45,952	10	0			
Less Arrears ...	75	0	0			
				45,877	10	0
„ VENDORS, being balance due to them with interest to date				51,250	0	0
„ 2nd Mortgagees „ „ ...				8,200	0	0
„ Anticipatory Call Account				1,033	9	0
„ Leicestershire Banking Company—						
Special Loan ...	1,500	0	0			
Overdraft	4,794	4	9			
				6,294	4	9
„ Bills Payable				644	18	5
„ Sundry Creditors				6,157	0	4
„ Accident Fund				171	11	2
„ Suspense Account				333	7	9
„ Balance from Profit and Loss Account ...				77	13	4
				£120,039	14	9

Cr.

	£	s.	d.	£	s.	d.
BY PURCHASE OF COLLIERY, viz., Land Leases, Buildings, &c....	77,000	0	0			
„ Plant	17,000	0	0			
	94,000	0	0			
Additions to Plant ...	272	13	1			
				94,272	13	1
„ Stock				5,353	13	0
„ Sundry Debtors				5,949	17	4
„ New Works Account—						
Colliery	5,519	11	3			
Brick Yard ..	2,486	14	9			
Fees for Kiln ...	100	0	0			
				8,106	6	0
„ Office Furniture				138	14	2
„ Rolling Stock	4,026	13	7			
Less depreciation as per Profit and Loss Account ...	201	6	7			
				3,825	7	0
„ Preliminary Expenses ...	2,368	17	1			
Less Written off ...	473	15	5			
				1,895	1	8
„ Cash in hand				498	2	6
				£120,039	14	9

I have examined the above Balance Sheet and Accounts, with the Vouchers from which they are compiled and certify the same to be correct.

August 19th, 1875. J. S. STALLARD, *Auditor.*

TRADING ACCOUNT.

12 Months ending 30th June, 1875.

Dr.

	£	s.	d.
To Wages	23,025	2	4
„ Salary and Commissions	722	12	3
„ Rents	475	0	0
„ Rates and Taxes	398	3	10
„ Sundry Charges	440	8	5
„ Loan of Locomotive	194	19	0
„ Keep of Horses	353	6	1
„ Materials and Stores	3,304	3	0
„ Railway Tonnage	9,545	10	2
„ Interest and Discount	89	13	8
„ Loss on Horses	96	10	0
„ Allowances	761	1	7
„ Petties	39	16	5
„ Stock 30th June, 1874	3,718	11	0
Gross Profit carried to Profit and Loss Account ...	6,063	7	2
	£49,228	4	11

Cr.

	£	s	d.
By Railway Sales	35,539	8	2
„ Pit Land Sales	1,849	0	0
„ Bagworth Wharf Sales	3,108	0	3
„ Old Materials	562	8	11
„ Wharfage on Wagons	2	2	0
„ Leading Workmen's Coals	1	13	0
„ Brick Yard Sales	5,210	7	0
„ Rent received for Pingle Wharf	8	12	8
„ Allotment Rents	36	2	0
„ Sale of Farm Produce and Implements ...	182	1	11
Stock 30th June, 1875	2,728	9	0
	£49,228	4	11

PROFIT AND LOSS ACCOUNT,

12 Months ending 30th June, 1875.

Dr.

	£	s.	d.
To Interest and Commission	4,621	10	9
„ Preliminary Expenses £2,368 17 1 ... 20 °/.	473	15	5
„ Law Expenses	459	14	3
„ Director's Fees, &c.	624	17	11
„ Salaries	579	9	8
„ Travelling Expenses	131	5	10
„ Printing and Stationery	36	19	10
„ Rent (London Office)	60	0	0
„ Advertising	160	5	0
„ Pingle Wharf	387	11	0
„ Bad Debts	600	0	0
„ Petties	48	11	2
„ Wagon Rents	410	8	7
„ Income Tax	108	6	8
„ Depreciation of Wagons	201	6	7
Nett Profit carried to Balance Sheet	77	13	4
	£8,981	16	0

Cr.

	£	s.	d.
By Balance Profit and Loss Account, 30th June, 1874	2,916	2	4
„ Balance being Profit brought from Trading Account	6,063	7	2
„ Transfer Fees	2	6	6
	£8,981	16	0

An Ibstock balance sheet for 1875. Among the company's expenses, a £96 10s "loss on horses" and "wagon rents" of £410 8s 7d.

contribute to the advantage of the colliery.

Dr. Thomson was, indeed, to contribute very quickly. By March 1875 his stake in the business had risen and he was appointed managing director on terms which gave him 10 per cent of the company's net profits.

He took half of all the allocated directors fees and out-of-pocket expenses incurred in travelling to and from Glasgow, the return trip costing £6. Even before taking up the post Dr. Thomson had impressed most of the directors with a series of ideas intended to improve profitability and to enhance the company's prospects.

He had recommended single-shift working to save cash and also suggested the closing down, at an estimated saving of £500 a year, of an office which the company operated in London. There was also a saving of £400 a year arising from the abrupt departure of the man he replaced.

With an eye on reducing debtors, the company also joined the Leicester Trade Protection Society, a debt collection business which it would still be using well into the middle of the next century.

Dr. Thomson would eventually become chairman, the first in a line of members of the Thomson family who were to exercise control and to hold influence over the Ibstock business for generations to come. His Wishaw operations, based on two principal collieries, would also continue, but only until the mid-1920s.

By the end of the 1870s Ibstock's performance was perking up. In 1879 its total assets stood at £135,000, including a figure of £563 6s for horses and ponies employed at the pit. Dr. Thomson, as set out in the terms of his employment, took £300 of the £600 available in directors' fees while colliery wages for the year were entered at £12,800.

Wages in the brickworks amounted to £1,147 according to accounts audited by Mr. Edward Roberts. Mr. Roberts had 10 years previously established his own accountancy firm which would, despite repeated changes of identity through successive mergers, continue to serve Ibstock for decades to come.

The business remained principally and overwhelmingly a colliery operation. While brick sales had been taking a growing share of the business - they were valued at £2,991 during the year - coal brought in over £27,000. Among the more unusual entries was a £200 credit towards "hay for the colliery."

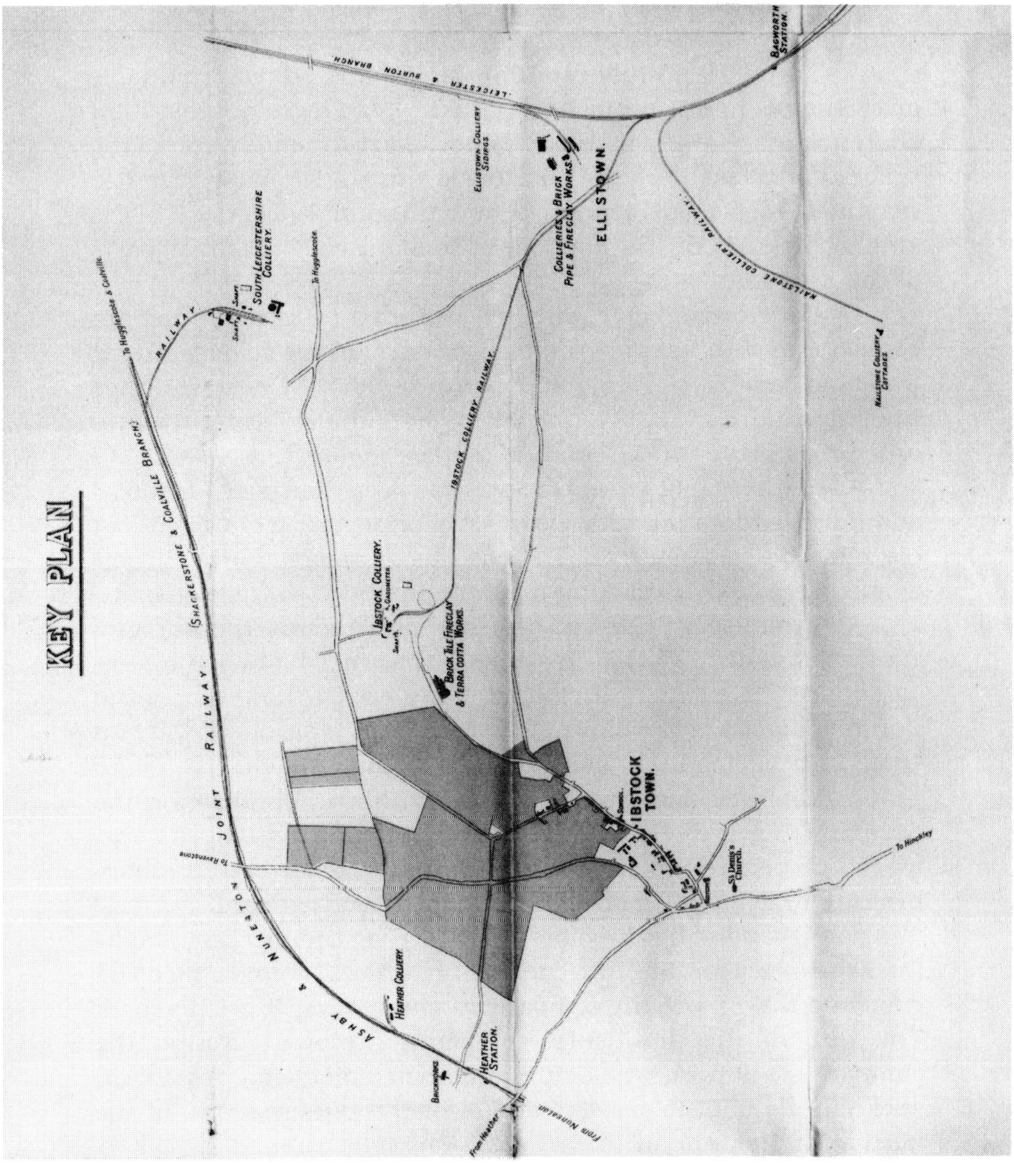

Ibstock 1891: An early plan of the district identifying the colliery and the branch railway line.

The 1879 annual profit of £2,496 13s 6d was creditable given the poor state of the coal industry. The directors told their shareholders that it was "scarcely necessary to remind you of the unfortunate fact that the coal trade during the past year has remained in a most depressed and unexampled state. This is amply borne out by the stoppage of so many collieries in all parts of the Kingdom."

Undeterred, the company continued to invest to remain competitive with its numerous neighbours. In the colliery output was now capable of being stepped up because of new workings underground. New subterranean roads had also been driven in order to improve ventilation and haulage.

Neither had the brickworks been ignored. Material additions and improvements to the brickyard were made "at considerable expense." There was, among other new acquisitions, a brickmaking machine intended to raise output.

Even so the directors had to report their regret "notwithstanding all their exertions" that they had been unable to obtain the results anticipated. They ended, however, on an optimistic note: "The quality of the articles now produced warrant them in believing in a future success in this branch."

Not everyone was as happy with the outlook for the company, however. Six shareholders, including Mr. James Cope, who had just resigned as a director, forced an extraordinary meeting to demand the resignation of the entire board.

Although the directors warned that the meeting, called for February 18, 1880, at the colliery offices, would "effect no good and may injure the company in many ways," it went ahead. The nub of the dissidents' complaints revolved around the company's financial well-being and their emergency resolution spoke of a complete reconstruction of the business and of the need for better management.

Their case collapsed, however, with the other shareholders present joining forces to vote down what they described as an "extremely damaging" attempt to censure the board. An amendment expressing the fullest confidence in the directors was passed by 14 votes to six.

By the early 1890s, as "the great depression" lifted, Ibstock's daily output of coal had reached 1,400 tons, aided by the commissioning of what is thought to have been the first mechanised coal-cutting machine in the region. Rail traffic to and from the pit increased significantly following the sinking in

1892 of a second main shaft. A deal was struck with William Whetstone, the former owner, who still leased some of his land to the colliery company. It reduced the royalty paid to him on top seam coal from 5d a ton to 3d a ton provided the company guaranteed a minimum output of 50,000 tons a year.

At the same time the directors' interest in developing the brickmaking side of the business was reinforced with a decision to erect three new kilns and two drying sheds at a cost of £500. The funds were to come from "a vigorous attempt to reduce the present, rather large stock at the brickyard." By now, there was also a modest output of salt-glazed pipes for use by builders.

Four years before the turn of the century the company moved to expand the core business further with a decision to purchase at auction the New Heather Colliery, a few miles from the Ibstock pit. The details, sent out to "colliery owners, capitalists, speculators and others," described the colliery as advantageously situated, with railway facilities to distribute coal as far as London.

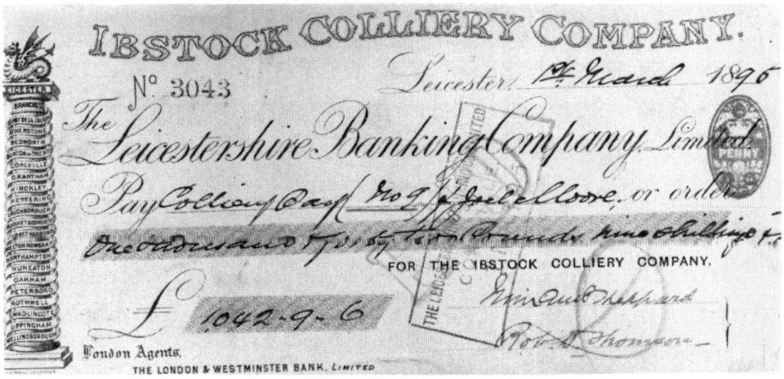

An Ibstock Colliery cheque dated 1895 and drawn on the Leicestershire Banking Company, the forerunner of the Midland Bank, with which Ibstock still conducts business.

The 484-acre site was held on leases with royalties of 3d a ton due to the landlord. The colliery was acquired by Ibstock at the auction, held at the Bull's Head Hotel in Leicester on January 21, 1896, but was never exploited by the new owners and would eventually be sold on to the National Coal Board for open-cast mining.

In the same year Mr. William Sheppard, who was married to Dr. Thomson's daughter Katherine, stepped down as chairman of Ibstock. He had assumed the post 10 years earlier after returning from living in Newfoundland following the death of Dr. Thomson.

He told his fellow directors that he intended to give one third of his shares in the business to his son William and to sell for £2,000 the remaining two-thirds to Dr. Thomson's two sons - both Ibstock directors - Samuel and Robert.

Samuel Thomson took the chair and, three years later, Ibstock dropped its partnership status to become a private limited company. One of the new chairman's challenges was to cope with his sister Katherine's own close interest in the business and her insistence on playing an influential role in its development.

Her forceful style at the time bred a certain amount of ill-feeling between the Thomson and Sheppard families, some of which would still be recalled, though not perpetuated, almost a century later.

The first shareholders' meeting of Ibstock Collieries Ltd., incorporated on August 4, 1899, took place two months later at the newly-constructed colliery head office. Shareholders in the new company were Robert and Samuel, William Sheppard Jnr., Mr. Charles Brown, a Glasgow stockbroker and friend of the Thomsons, Mr. Walter Whetstone and Mr. William Patchett Frost, partners in a firm of Leicester solicitors, and Mr. Clarendon Hyde, a London barrister.

By now Robert had taken over as chairman from his brother and was also elected joint managing director with William Sheppard on salaries of £600 a year. Edward Roberts and his partner J. H. Baker were re-appointed as auditors on a fee of £60 per annum. Mr. Baker joined the board.

In 1903 Samuel died, leaving Robert, a lawyer by training, as the sole remaining family representative among the directors. They expressed their profound regret at the loss of a man who had given the colliery his "untiring devotion" since 1884.

With the Victorian era finally at an end, making way for the pomp and glitter of Edwardian prosperity, companies like Ibstock had grounds for believing the future looked good. Though the colliery operation's profitability was fragile - several annual losses were recorded in the early years of the new century - the brickworks managed to achieve small but welcome profits.

But the nation's industrial base was expanding again. Exports of coal and machinery were growing and there was a fresh upsurge in unionism which was to lead to the formation of the Labour Party.

Although Ibstock remained primarily and overwhelmingly a colliery operation, mining and distributing its coal to customers in the West Midlands and beyond, the spin-off operations were by now becoming more important.

By 1907, as an outbreak of Glanders disease hit the colliery's pit ponies leaving 10 dead and frightening local farmers into moving their cattle away from the area, the directors' thoughts were turning with increasing regularity to other areas of potential business. The mining operation was still producing patchy profits while demand for bricks and pipes from the local construction industry was steadily rising.

Coal production at the end of the first decade of the 20th Century - shortly before a national miners' strike over wages brought most of the industry to a standstill for three months - was running at 300,000 tons annually.

But the output of bricks, unpredictable in quality yet in high demand from a hungry local building trade, was growing. By the out-break of the First World War about three million bricks a year were being turned out of Ibstock's beehive kilns and trundled away from the site.

Though the immediate future held nothing but carnage, chaos and commercial disruption, the post-war years were to see the modest Leicestershire business begin to evolve in a way its creators could never have imagined.

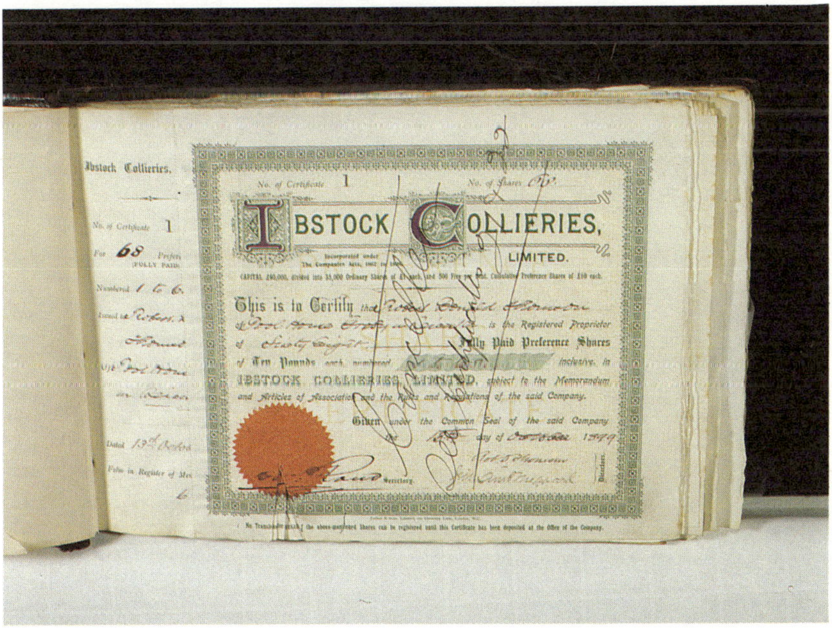

An Ibstock Collieries share certificate, dated 1899 and made out in the name of Robert Donald Thomson, of Pool House, Groby, Leicestershire, the chairman of the company. Robert was the son of the first of the Thomson family line of Ibstock caretakers and grandfather of the current chairman.

2

Conflict at home and abroad

IBSTOCK Colliery itself was to bear some of the wounds of the Great War. By May 1915 the directors had to record the death in action of Samuel Pestell Thomson, the chairman's nephew, who fell in France fighting with the Leicestershire Yeomanry.

Samuel had only been appointed to the board in March 1914 along with Robert Hyde, a son of the chairman. Fate was also to deal a cruel blow to Robert Hyde himself, though it would not prevent him from playing a highly decisive role in the future development of the company.

The outbreak of hostilities saw both the railways and the coal mines brought under Government control. By the time the war was over the state actually owned 250 mines or quarries, though Ibstock was not large enough to have to sacrifice its own independence. As volunteers joined the army the Government faced a labour shortage to the extent that more than 200,000 men employed in the mines - equivalent to an output of 60 million tons of coal a year - heeded the call to fight for King and country in the first year of the war.

Strikes were forbidden by law from 1915, though the need to maintain armaments production meant that, when miners in south Wales withdrew their labour later the same year,

Government intervention ensured they were back at work within five days.

At Ibstock production was maintained, despite the absence of the significant number of workers who had enlisted. Such was the level of sales to industrial customers who were hard-pressed to contribute to the national war effort that the colliery shareholders enjoyed dividend payments - by no means guaranteed in earlier years - throughout the duration of the conflict.

Within months of the end of the war the board was setting new production targets for coal output, encouraged by a Lloyd George coalition Government intent upon post-war social and industrial reconstruction.

A daily target of 1,300 tons was fixed but, to the obvious impatience of the directors, the workforce failed to deliver. As part of the effort to boost production Mr. J. J. Torrance had been appointed as colliery manager at an annual salary of £350 "with free house, coals and light" to work under Mr. William Ramsay, the general manager. But absenteeism and illness ensured that output doggedly refused to rise above 1,100 tons daily.

Despite an increase in the workforce following the return of servicemen intent upon achieving the better way of life they had been promised, the directors were left to remark that output per man per shift was "very far from what it should be." Every effort, they intoned, would have to be made to see that production was improved.

Though it could not appreciate it at the time, the board's problems with the colliery workforce were only a taste of what was to come. The coal industry was to become a classic example of the post-war failure of British industry and it was soon to find itself at the centre of a national crisis.

By 1919 the Miners Federation was demanding a 30 per cent pay rise, a six-hour day and nationalisation of the nation's mines. The Government refused the demands, sparking off a pit stoppage. Lloyd George acted swiftly, however, appointing a coal industry commission to inquire into wages, hours and the issue of state ownership.

The commission finally recommended nationalisation, a move which drove Ibstock's chairman publicly to express his "gravest apprehension" at the prospect of a measure which would "circumscribe the scope for individual initiative and enterprise and was directly opposed to the general interests of the nation."

All the miners were to get, however, was a new Coal Act which introduced a seven-hour day, and a modest increase in wages.

The chairman, whose surname by now had become Hyde-Thomson in order to preserve the name of Eva Hyde, his wife, attacked the Government. It had been too ready, he claimed, to establish the commission in the face of the "threatening attitude" adopted by the so-called "triple alliance,"' which had been formed by the railwaymen, the transport workers and the miners to fight for improved conditions.

He claimed the immediate result of the commission had been a further increase in absenteeism and lower output per shift. The men, he said, were now able to "live up to their former standard of comfort without being under the necessity of exerting themselves to the same extent as formerly."

No doubt the directors believed their workers were treated comparably well and that, in return, their best endeavours were expected. They had supported the formation of a miners' welfare club, through which each member contributed 2d a week to the Leicester Royal Infirmary and Saturday Hospital in order to ensure some limited form of medical treatment was available when necessary.

There were also organised trips to seaside resorts in order to allow the workers to blow away the coal dust and breathe in fresh air. Each year the club would vote on the destination. Blackpool invariably won.

The company had also established its own accident fund, which was ready to pay accident benefit and would provide £30 on the death of an employee, though only £16 for a wife. There were the inevitable abuses, like the case of one Jesse Morley who asked for funeral expenses to bury his wife. The directors were informed that the lady in question was not his spouse so "the matter would not be entertained." Workers would also have benefit denied them if they breached the rules by getting drunk.

Ibstock's financial position was not helped by the continuing Government-imposed price controls on coal, though there was some relief in the summer of 1919 when the colliery received notification from the Controller of Mines which allowed an increase of 6s a ton in pit head prices.

But within months the chairman had more to complain about to his fellow directors, now joined by Mr. Cater Hyde-Thomson, one of his sons, and Mr. William Heath Eves, a relative of the chairman. The company, he said, protested strongly at the

Government's decision to enact legislation which would place a ceiling on profits per ton of coal sold. In Ibstock's eyes the move effectively confiscated 50 per cent of the profits to which the company was entitled under the existing Coal Mines Control Agreement, which set selling prices.

The chairman warned solemnly: "So long as the coal trade is under Government control it is essential, in order to prevent the key industry of the country from being crippled, that at least the pre-War standard of profit should be guaranteed to the coal owners."

At the end of 1919 William Sheppard, a director since the business took on limited company status and who had been primarily responsible for the brick-making operations, died. Only a few months before, his wife Katherine had also died.

Early in the following year his seat on the board was taken by Donald Sheppard, one of William's four sons, who had stayed on in the army after the end of the War. He had won a degree in electrical and mechanical engineering from Cambridge University and was the only son to express an interest in joining the business. He would eventually become deputy chairman.

With "undivided responsibility" for the management of the company now resting with the chairman, his salary was raised to £1,500 a year. Along with the other board members, his appointment qualified him for certain perks, notably "coal and firewood, each to have sufficient for one establishment." The fuel was not free, however, but made available at concessionary rates. Coal cost 2s 6d a ton and firewood the same, though delivery charges were waived.

In 1921 the coal mines were handed back to their owners by the Government, which led to immediate and severe wage cuts for the workers. The miners rejected them and withdrew their labour. At Ibstock the colliery, which by now employed several thousand men, came to a standstill. The directors were given a report of the "great strike" and heard a report from the Leicestershire Coal Owners Association on the progress of talks with miners' leaders in London.

The strike was short-lived, however, following the failure of other members in the "triple alliance" to back the miners' action. The planned show of solidarity collapsed and the alliance was derisively dubbed the "cripple alliance."

A few months later Ibstock's chairman died suddenly while on holiday in Cornwall and it fell to his son Robert Hyde to take the chair. The task would have seemed great enough for a man who, after an education at Harrow and Oxford University, had trained and qualified for the Bar and who had shown little interest in getting to grips with managing a colliery and brick-making business. For Robert Hyde, who had been totally blinded while fighting on the Somme with the 9th Battalion, the Rifle Brigade, the challenge must have appeared monumental.

The chairman's son had gone to war shortly after the birth of his own first son and was struck down by a bullet at Flers in September 1916. He lay in a shell hole for three days before being rescued and brought back to England, a crippled 26-year old whose future must have seemed bleak and uncertain.

But his own determined spirit and an extremely supportive wife and family helped a courteous and caring man re-establish a sense of purpose as well as a will to overcome his appalling disability. With his brother Cater at his side to oversee the colliery operation he began to fill his father's shoes.

Donald Sheppard, one of Ibstock's directors from 1920 until after the Second World War. He was the grandson of the original Dr. Samuel Thomson whose daughter Katherine married William Sheppard, Ibstock's chairman in the ebbing years of the 19th Century.

In 1918 Robert Hyde penned a poem to his younger brother, part of which read:

"Now you direct the collieries,
Just think, my boy, how nice it is;
You'll turn up once a month with me.
We'll make no sort or kind of fuss,
The wheels go round in spite of us."

Cater's contribution, however, was to be cut short by his untimely death in January 1923 after suffering from tuberculosis for 10 years.

His brother could hardly have taken on such responsibilities at a worse time in the coal industry's history. Quite apart from the industrial unrest which continued to characterise its activities, mining was suffering from rising foreign competition, especially from Poland and from the Germans, who were making some reparations for war damage in consignments of coal.

Major industrial users of coal were in decline and the industry's productivity was falling. By now there were about 2,500 mines owned by 1,400 companies. Around 300 of them produced 85 per cent of total UK output and overmanning was rife, with the total number of coal industry employees having swollen by 50 per cent in the previous decade.

One of the new chairman's first tasks was to preside over the voluntary liquidation of the Wishaw Coal Company, the Scottish colliery operation which had survived as a separate entity since the days of Dr. Thomson.

Still controlled by the family, Wishaw's best days were over and the business was now rapidly running down. Two of the collieries were sold off and, by the start of 1923 - which saw the first, short-lived Labour Government under Ramsay MacDonald - the business was being wound up. At the end the business held funds of just over £85,000. Ibstock's chairman had greater personal and commercial challenges ahead. Unlike his father, who had travelled by pony cart from the colliery to his home at Pool House in the nearby village of Groby, Robert Hyde lived in London, where he could best be encouraged to mix, make friends and come to terms with his blindness.

Undaunted, he began to make the long journey alone from his home in Kensington via St. Pancras station to Leicester. On his arrival he would be met and driven to Ibstock, where he would check the books and receive progress reports from Mr. Torrance, the colliery manager, and Mr. Joseph Sparrow, who was manager of the still-expanding brickworks.

"J.J." Sparrow had started with the company as a lad of 13 after he had been admonished by Robert Hyde's father for throwing a bottle over a wall at the chairman's feet.

So impressed was the then chairman with Sparrow's handling of a tricky situation that he offered him a job. The boy began at once as a pit pony driver and he would go on to play a pre-eminent role in the future development of the company.

Among the chairman's early decisions was the

appointment of a travelling salesmen - at a salary of £5 a week - and of another to be based in London, on 1d-a-ton commission. Almost at once a salesmen was appointed for the brick and pipeworks department and in 1923 the company's reducing dependence on its coal mining activities was reflected in its membership of the Sanitary Pipe Association.

If little thought had so far been given by the directors to the possibility of withdrawing from the mining business, impending events were to lead to a dramatic change in direction for Ibstock.

Unrest in the coal mining industry bubbled away and in, 1925, the restoration of the gold standard had disastrous effects on coal exports. At the same time a Government subsidy which had enabled wage levels in the industry to be maintained came to an end and the pit owners demanded new wage cuts - by up to £1 10s a week - and longer working hours.

Mr "J.J." Sparrow, perhaps the longest-serving employee of the company who started as a pit pony driver and retired as a director.

Confrontation was again in the air with the miners, having renewed their pleas for nationalisation, adopting the slogan "not a penny off the pay, not a second on the day." By 1926 the Trades Union Congress was supporting the miners, a lock-out at the pits began at the end of April and the General Strike followed at once.

Nine days later the unions caved in to what was virtually unconditional surrender, although the trouble in the coal fields was far from over. From the first day of May the miners at Ibstock walked out and, although some of the staff tried their hands at moving wagon loads of coal away from the pithead, production ceased. The pit remained silent and unproductive until the end of August, with the men, forced back to work by the suffering of their families, gradually returning at the end of August, several weeks before the national stoppage was over.

The board was told that the underground workings had been maintained in a reasonably satisfactory condition during the stoppage and that resumption of mining would not create too many problems.

While the pit had remained idle, however, the demand for sanitary pipes and bricks had held up well and, by the start of 1927, the company embarked on the manufacture of roofing tiles. Power for the new plant was to be purchased from the Warwickshire and Leicestershire Power Company.

In the same year the company's profits reached just over £24,000, a performance which was regarded as highly unsatisfactory and which would have been worse but for the contribution from brick and pipe sales.

Demand for coal remained extremely depressed, particularly from export markets, and the onset of a world economic crisis was to leave British industry in general and Ibstock in particular facing a bleak future.

"Annie," the faithful locomotive which completed 60 years' service at Ibstock before being scrapped in 1957.

The company decided to give up what had become an increasingly unequal struggle. On October 24, 1928 the directors met at the St. Pancras Hotel in London to hear a report which had been commissioned from Mr. R.A. Tomlinson, a well-known mining engineer from Doncaster.

Increasingly concerned about the lack of profitability of a

mining operation based on thin seams of coal, which could not be worked efficiently, and alarmed at the outlook for sales, the board had called for an honest assessment of the company's prospects.

Mr. Tomlinson's report only confirmed what the directors already knew; the pit was uneconomic and should be permanently closed. It was not so much a "life or death" decision as the board was confident the business could be kept going. But the chairman saw no point in fighting the facts and the only decision left to take was how quickly to shut the colliery and throw several thousand men out of work.

For such a sensitive and considerate man the decision was a difficult one but the engineer's report left few options. It suggested that losses per ton were likely to reach at least 1s 6d over the next few months, representing a total cash loss of anything up to £10,000.

Over the same period, the profits from the pipe and brick works would amount to £2,500, leaving a net overall loss in the region of £7,500.

The directors concluded, without much debate: "After a careful examination of the market possibilities and the heavy losses that have been, and are being, sustained we feel bound in the interests of the shareholders to recommend that the closure of the pits should be immediate and the necessary notices should be issued forthwith."

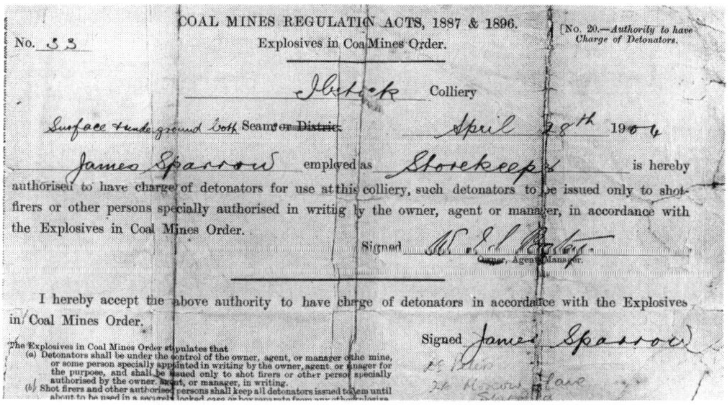
COAL MINES REGULATION ACTS, 1887 & 1896.
Explosives in Coal Mines Order.

[No. 20.—*Authority to have Charge of Detonators.*

No. 33

Ibstock Colliery

Surface + underground both Seam ~~or District~~ April 28th 1904

James Sparrow employed as Storekeeper is hereby authorised to have charge of detonators for use at this colliery, such detonators to be issued only to shot-firers or other persons specially authorised in writing by the owner, agent or manager, in accordance with the Explosives in Coal Mines Order.

Signed W. E. S. Bart
Owner, Agent, Manager.

I hereby accept the above authority to have charge of detonators in accordance with the Explosives in Coal Mines Order.

Signed James Sparrow

The Explosives in Coal Mines Order stipulates that
(a) Detonators shall be under the control of the owner, agent, or manager of the mine, or some person specially appointed in writing by the owner, agent or manager for the purpose, and shall be issued only to shot firers or other persons specially authorised by the owner, agent, or manager, in writing.
(b) Shot firers and other authorised persons shall keep all detonators issued to them until about to be used in a securely locked case or box separate from any other explosive

Authorisation, dated 1904, under the Coal Mines Regulation Acts for "J.J." Sparrow to handle explosives for extracting coal at Ibstock.

The board, in an attempt to soften the blow for its workers, said that it would make available £7,500 to help in cases of "severe distress" brought about by the closure. By early 1929, the year in which Mr. John Walton became the latest in a succession of company secretaries, some of them bearing highly memorable names such as Mr. Death and Mr. Friend, the mining business which had first brought Ibstock Collieries into being was shut down.

At first the chairman had given some thought to closing the business altogether but some of his colleagues - notably Donald Sheppard, by now holding the rank of Major - believed there could be a good future for the brickworks. The latter view won the day and, for Ibstock, a new and very different future lay ahead.

3

A total transformation

THE 1930s began with unemployment at 2,500,000 and the British economy still struggling with deep recession. Public expenditure had been cut and building activity was at low levels but, even so, Ibstock was trying to plan positively for a future as a producer of bricks, pipes and tiles.

For the first time the directors began to consider the purchase of other businesses as a way of expanding their own operation. Although sales were rising they remained well below the levels the company believed to be attainable.

The first opportunity to grow by acquisition came in the summer of 1932 when the owners of the Coalville Brick Company, a modest brick production yard a couple of miles north of Ibstock, paid a visit to see the chairman.

The Coalville operation was struggling and its directors named a price at which it was prepared to sell out to its bigger, stronger neighbour. The Ibstock board, however, believed the price being asked was too high and the business on offer was not sufficiently attractive. The offer was politely declined.

With gross sales of its products - predominantly bricks - now running at around £70,000 a year, profitability was improving. By the autumn of 1933 the directors were told that

Ibstock's liquid assets were looking healthy but that they could not all be usefully employed in the business as it stood. Despite various approaches and proposals, the company had been unable to find acceptable ways of locating any new investments which were secure and which would help boost its customer base.

Attention turned to modernising and expanding the company's Ibstock plant, which offered plenty of room for improvement. The works must have appeared Dickensian, with tubs of clay moving on an endless chain to the mill top, where it was tipped, crushed by rollers and ground by "kibblers" ready for shaping and cutting into bricks.

As for the kilns there were no mechanical means of monitoring the fire temperatures, with the the colour of the flames telling an experienced eye all it needed to know. No bricks were kept in stock. As the bricks were loaded - the closer to the centre of the kiln the hotter they became - straw was placed between them to prevent damage. On occasions it would ignite and lorries would be lost in the ensuing inferno.

By the end of 1933 the management had called in Mr. Arthur Brown, a London-based consulting engineer to appraise the production facilities and to make recommendations for improving efficiency and stepping up output.

Mr. Brown's principal conclusion was that the works were run "as well as possible" but that they were largely out of date. His report disclosed the limited manufacture, alongside the normal production run, of an alternative rustic brick, though he was not overly impressed. He suggested that the addition of crushed flint or granite would improve its appearance.

The plant, according to Mr. Brown, was annually producing about three million bricks and five million tiles and pipes but it was under-utilised, consumed extravagant tonnages of coal and made inefficient use of kiln space. The obvious, though unwritten, conclusion, was that Ibstock had to invest in a new production plant.

The board agreed and decided to embark on an ambitious investment programme intended to establish the business on a bigger scale. Just as it acted the building industry began to emerge from the gloom and, by the spring of 1934, a wave of new, private housing development boosted demand for building materials.

Speculative housing developers, encouraged by the ready availability of mortgages of up to 95 per cent of the purchase price, erected homes for sale at prices of between £500-£600. The public responded with enthusiasm and the building industry took off.

In July 1934 Ibstock signed an agreement with Gibbons Brothers of Dudley in Worcestershire for the construction of a Monnier kiln, one of the first tunnel kilns in Britain for the production of brick, at a cost of £8,000. Such was its rarity - the bricks moved through the kiln on cars instead of remaining stationary - that Ibstock had to agree with the makers to allow other interested customers to visit the plant and see it in action.

An early picture of steam wagons and crew at Aldridge Colliery, advertising "best deep" coals as well as bricks and tiles. Ibstock would acquire the Aldridge Brick Tile & Coal business in 1965.

The 297ft.-long kiln, with a peak temperature of 1,040 degrees centigrade, represented the company's biggest single investment - partly financed by the sale of shares - and would enable production to rise to nine million bricks a year.

The new plant, to become known as the North Works, eventually came on stream in 1935, though not without some problems.

One of the driving forces behind this and many of the subsequent Ibstock developments was "J.J." Sparrow, whose position as works manager enabled him and his family to live in "Redlands," a Victorian house on the edge of the plant close to the Leicester Road.

His daughter Dorothy, who was also to work for the company, well remembers the day when her aunt stared, horrified, through a bedroom window to see the metal framework for the new kiln collapse like a pack of cards.

"J.J.", always sporting a suit and watch-chain, was

notorious around the works for signalling his daily mood by the type of hat he chose to wear; a trilby meant good news and a cap meant trouble. There can be little doubt which choice of headgear he donned as he marched across to the kiln site, his dog "Nigger" beside him, on that particular day.

The chairman made regular visits to keep in touch with progress, sometimes bringing with him his nine-year-old son Paul, who was occasionally given a ride on one of the steam engines and sometimes permitted to blow the whistle.

The company was now also taking other decisions to reflect both its changing character and its growing size. Before 1934 was over it had rented an office and some showroom space at 11, Kelso Place in Kensington, close to the chairman's London home. It also opened a railway depot nearby to handle the growing volume of sales being made to a hungry building industry.

The Aldridge plant, as seen in 1934 from the nearby Empire Works.

The new offices were, in November of the same year, the setting for an extraordinary general meeting of the company at which it was agreed to change the name of Ibstock Collieries to Ibstock Brick & Tile Company. The metamorphosis was completed with the new name taking effect on January 1, 1935.

Although the company was now growing, the management team, still housed in its sparse bungalow office close to the new works, remained small. Each morning Jack Gilliver, the office boy, would ensure that the day's post was on the company secretary's desk early and that four buckets of coal were filled and ready to keep the office fire going for the day.

John Walton was an assiduous company secretary for whom economy was the key, though his aversion to spending money often incurred the anger and disbelief of his colleagues.

The Walton work ethic meant, for example, that new pencils would only be provided when the old stub was handed in as proof that extravagance was being curbed. He would light his cigarettes in the office fire rather than use a match, and he hated to see unused paper being used for scrap.

Annoying as his obsessions might have appeared, he instilled in his colleagues the need for a small business to make economies, a principle which was to characterise its progress for years to come.

Also in the office was John Grover, the sales manager. A dominant personality, few of his colleagues liked him, but none could challenge his sales skills or fail to admire the restless energy of a man who lived on his nerves. Always in early, he would court customers by telephone or in person, utilising his £500 a year expense allowance. Between sales sorties he could usually be found with his feet up on a paper-strewn desk and with a cigarette in his mouth.

Grover, a product of a minor public school and Sandhurst, had a clear vision of the market which he believed Ibstock could carve out for itself. He saw no reason why it could not be achieved and went for it. There is no doubt that, without his drive and imagination, the company would not have developed in the way it eventually would.

Grover had some help in the shape of travelling salesmen like Leslie Truelove, who would eventually join the board, and Reg Baker, the archetypal traveller, permanently clad in a dark suit with gold watchchain and bowler hat.

But it was "J.J." who dominated the office and the Ibstock works. A father-figure to many of those with whom he worked, he could invoke equal amounts of fear and affection from those around him. To the directors, and to Robert Hyde Hyde-Thomson in particular, his sound common sense, long experience and wise counsel was invaluable.

A self-taught man, he kept an ever-watchful eye on his workforce. He was both tough and kind; on some cold days he would send for packets of Woodbines to hand out to the men; on others he would upbraid them for wasting time by lighting fires.

On occasions Sparrow could be spotted in the yard on a Sunday morning - the day reserved for hand-loading the lorries

An early photograph of Ibstock Number One Pit, complete with winding gear and empty railway trucks.

The earliest picture of Ibstock South Works, photographed in the 1930s.

The North Works kiln photographed shortly after its completion in 1934.

- sharing a breakfast with men who had cooked eggs and bacon on the back of a shovel. But if an employee complained he was doing the work of two men the works manager was quite likely to reply: "Give me the name of the other one so I can sack him."

Directly answerable to Sparrow were three foremen, Tom Findlay, Tom Crofts and Tom Iliffe, who would watch each morning as the men and women picked up their tally - a small, numbered disc which registered their arrival for work - and headed off to their jobs.

Late arrivals, regardless of the excuse, could be sent home and might lose a day's pay. The working day stretched from early morning until 6.30 in the evenings, with half a day off on Saturdays.

Throughout the 1930s the chairman continued to make the journey to and from his home in Kensington, always seated in the railway restaurant car and in the same position so that the employee meeting him would know where to stand on the platform to await his arrival at Leicester.

An Ibstock staff dinner in 1937. Among those seated are Robert Hyde Hyde-Thomson and "J.J." Sparrow.

The manner in which he coped with his disability was a source of admiration to everyone at Ibstock, though to most of them he remained a distant figure to be respected rather than befriended.

People like Leslie Truelove remember being twice interviewed by the chairman before realising that he was blind. Others recall how his enhanced sense of hearing could detect faults at the works before sighted employees were aware of them. Wooden models would be built of new plant so that the chairman could feel the company's proposed developments.

On many of his visits to Ibstock he continued to be accompanied by his wife Joan or his son Paul, who would read him the Times leader or details from the company's accounts. He was a very good listener, anxious to hear the views of those around him and to do what was best for the future of the company.

By 1937 the company had decided to build its own modest offices on a patch of railway land close to Kensington High Street at Wright's Lane. It agreed to pay £1 13s 4d a year for the lease and opened a London office account which was initially credited with £50. As war in Europe approached the company appeared to be in good shape. Sales were strong - Sparrow invariably told the men they would be working until ten o'clock at night to help boost production - and good profits were being notched up. Construction work on the local aerodrome being prepared as a launching pad for bombing raids against Hitler provided an added boost to sales.

At the outbreak of hostilities in 1939 the company was producing a rising number of facing bricks, tiles and sanitary pipeware products. In a decade it had transformed itself from a colliery to an increasingly well-known supplier of building materials, though no-one was prepared to guess how it would fare over the next 10 years.

For Ibstock the war years meant trying to get on with business as best as possible. Those working in the brick industry found themselves classified as a reserved occupation; their work was considered as important a part of the war effort as any other. Though some went off to fight - about 10 per cent of the men joined the forces - they were not obliged to do so.

The Ministry of Defence became a principal customer but, in the midst of destruction, some building activity continued. While the North Works maintained production throughout the war, the South Works was closed down. Inevitably brick stocks mounted and, at times, it seemed as though it was pipe sales which kept the business going.

In an address to the workers the chairman said the company's fate was in the hands of the Government. Everything would be done, he stressed, to obtain a share of whatever trade was going and to ensure the works were kept ready for a full resumption of output at the first opportunity.

There were few other signs of the impact of war on the

brick plant, though the company faced something of a challenge in blacking out the brick kilns so as not to assist enemy bombers. The closure of the hand-made tile-making operation and the conversion of the shed into a hostel for displaced Italians, Czechs and Turks provided further evidence that, beyond Ibstock, the world was in turmoil.

For a short while also a number of prisoners of war were held at Ibstock. Their arrival provided a potent reminder that some of their own colleagues were being held captive in Europe and there were attempts to send them food parcels and money.

Regularly the workers found themselves being marshalled together for instruction on defence from the Home Guard. There were, for example, sessions on the use of a Bren gun, which on one occasion at least was quickly terminated when an over-enthusiastic trainee fired off a shot into the pipeworks at the end of the canteen. The invaders, however, were never to confront Ibstock's doughty defence forces.

There were, nevertheless, casualties among the workforce. The accident club, which reminded Ibstock's men and women to carry gas masks at all times, quite regularly recorded the payment of cash sums to the dependents of men killed in action - £7 10s for a single man and £15 for someone with a family.

The chairman, still often accompanied by Paul, continued to travel backwards and forwards from London to the works. They would often stay at the Grand Hotel in Leicester where, in the winter months, Paul would huddle up against a one-bar gas fire and read out the details of invoices to a man with a memory well capable of assessing how they compared with those of the previous month. His father's thoroughness was an exercise in financial expediency which would serve the young man well in the future.

On occasions Paul would also go with his father to the Leicester offices of the company's auditors, their name by now having changed to Baker Brothers, Halford & Co. as the result of subsequent amalgamations. He remembers long conversations between his father and Everard Chamberlain, the firm's senior partner and an old friend, which were not best calculated to inspire in him an interest in the business of brickmaking.

He well recalls, however, the framed copy of the accounts of Ibstock Colliery, possibly its oldest client, which hung on Chamberlain's office wall. They were for 1877 and showed

Ibstock's assets standing at £131,175 14s 7d.

It never occurred to Paul that, before long, he would become the principal architect of the business whose affairs, at that time, held no interest for him. A Harrow boy, where he became head of school, his thoughts were of fighting for King and country, but the conflict was to end in his last term and he would be forced to rethink his plans.

With the war over the Government arranged for the early release from service of bricklayers and allied tradesmen and training establishments were set up throughout the country to help prepare for a wave of new post-war construction. No special arrangements were made, however, to release personnel to make the bricks. Some of the company's former employees returned from action to take up their old jobs. Among the directors and management Donald Sheppard came back a Colonel and John Grover returned a Lieutenant Colonel. "J.J." Sparrow had, by now, served the company for 50 years and was appointed a director before relinquishing his daily duties at the works.

There would be other appointments to the board in the aftermath of the war. The company was anxious to make up for lost time and lost business and, before 1945 was over, the directors were discussing the possibility of erecting new kiln capacity to boost production.

Conscious of the difficulties which lay ahead in recruiting more workers, the company also began to consider the creation of a housing association to build homes which it could rent to employees as an incentive.

In 1946, with Robert Hyde Hyde-Thomson celebrating 25 years as Ibstock chairman, work began on the construction of a 20-chamber kiln at the South Works, increasing brick-producing capacity from around 10 million bricks a year to 18 million. The project was disrupted, however, by a shortage of bricklayers and of steel, which was in strictly limited supply.

There were also early post-war problems with the quality of bricks being produced, invariably because Government restrictions on the unnecessary movement of materials meant Ibstock had to rely totally on local supplies of softer coal which burned quickly and meant bricks were often insufficiently fired. Inferior quality was not a characteristic associated with Ibstock facing bricks and there were numerous complaints from customers around the country.

Leslie Truelove, by now London manager with a London

salary of £600 a year, was at the sharp end: "The complaints came in thick and fast. Some of them were serious in the extreme and considerable costs were at stake.

"I had to make all sorts of unusual arrangements to clear things up. Some buildings had to have bricks cut out and replaced with blue bricks to avoid a collapse. Some work was pulled down and, in many cases, bricks taken back off sites. It was a dreadful, physical gallop, tearing all over the south and east of England to visit affected sites." An improvement in coal supplies resolved the situation quite quickly and Ibstock's good name had been only temporarily tarnished.

In 1947 Paul's older brother John joined the board as a non-executive director along with David Sheppard, an old war-time chum who was the Sandhurst-trained son of the Colonel. Another new boardroom recruit was Douglas Eves, the son of William Heath Eves and a second cousin to Paul. Between them, the Hyde-Thomson, Sheppard and Eves families controlled the business and all three were now represented in the boardroom.

Hard work at the clay face in 1945.

John had won one of the first Military Crosses awarded during the war, although he would go on to spend much of it in captivity, despite making several escapes. Douglas had been badly wounded serving in Holland. To both men their appointments were a means of ensuring continuing family representation within the company. Douglas, however, had been spotted by the chairman as someone who could make an active contribution to the development of the company.

Before the war he had visited Ibstock as a teenager,

travelling from Rugby where he was at school. By 1947 he had become a school master at Repton, from where he would travel to occasional board meetings.

It was during dinner at the Bath Club in London's West End that the chairman told Douglas he was anxious to see him play a significant role in the company. The advice was to train as a barrister and gradually to involve himself more with the business.

As for Paul, his next step was national service, following his father into the Rifle Brigade. A career in the diplomatic service, possibly attaining ambassadorial level, seemed the most likely path ahead. It was not to be.

4

Towering ambitions

HAVING thoroughly enjoyed his spell of national service, based during 1947 and 1948 in Vienna where he acted as aide-de-camp to General Jack Winterton, Austria's deputy commissioner, Paul Hyde-Thomson went to Oxford to read economics at Christ Church. His pride was about to take its first fall.

The young Hyde-Thomson had not been accustomed to failing in anything, so it came as a complete shock when he was subsequently turned down for entrance to the world of diplomacy. His undoing was largely at the hands of Lady Violet Bonham Carter, daughter of the former Liberal prime minister Herbert Asquith and herself a recent president of the Liberal Party. As a member of the interview panel she cross-examined him closely on the economics of life in the East End of London. It was not his best subject.

By now, however, he was preparing to marry and his future wife's guardians demonstrated an understandable concern over his ability to take care of her. A degree would not in itself secure much of a future and it was agreed that Paul would seek qualification as a chartered accountant in order to give him an entrée into the business world.

In 1950, the year in which Colonel Sheppard, the company's deputy chairman, died, Paul married Zoë d'Erlanger. Directly after his honeymoon he was articled to Mr. Donovan Touche, of George A. Touche & Co., a medium-sized firm of accountants with offices in Laurence Pountney Hill in the City of London which would eventually become one of Britain's largest accountancy firms.

Three years later he would qualify as an accountant. At Ibstock both John Walton and John Grover joined the board.

By now the first homes to be built at Ibstock by the newly-formed housing association - at a cost of £1,250 each - were completed and occupied. Twenty semi-detached houses in three different designs were to be erected, all of them built - naturally enough - with the company's own products. The range of facing bricks available was still very limited and the houses were built with Silver Grey hand- made and Buff Rustics. They were roofed with clay tiles from pre-War stock and were drained with salt-glazed clay pipes produced by the company.

There were strict rules for the tenants of what were effectively "tied" homes. Rent was one week in advance, lost keys would be replaced at a charge of 2s, the gardens had to be tidy and no poultry or pigeons would be allowed. The estate, standing back from the Leicester-Ibstock Road, was quickly dubbed "Sparrow's barracks."

In 1951, Paul's brother John married and decided to join the Kenya Rifles. Paul was appointed an alternate director in his place. But within three months of John's departure for a new life, and at just 34 years of age, he died in Uganda. In October the same year Paul was elected to take his brother's place.

In the same year the company took on the latest in a line of works managers who had briefly held the demanding job since "J.J." Sparrow stepped down. They had included George Elliot, Arthur Clamp and John Wilson but now came Jim Donaldson, a stern Scot from Barrhead on the edge of Glasgow, who had nearly joined Ibstock a couple of years earlier. A graduate from Glasgow University who had also spent time at Stoke-on-Trent College of Ceramics, Donaldson was then employed at the Doulton pipeworks in Erith, Kent.

Having heard that the post of works manager was available, he had expressed an interest and had been shown round by "J.J." But he was so appalled at the condition of the works - "such an untidy, filthy place" - that he politely declined the offer of work.

In his report of the interview to the chairman "J.J." stated: "Mr. Donaldson expressed great surprise at the untidiness of the works generally and said he felt it would be a reduction in status for him to take the job."

Even so, by the end of 1950 his father's illness meant Donaldson had himself moved to the Midlands. He renewed his contacts with the company and, finding that the chairman had left the post open in the hope of eventually attracting him, started work at Ibstock in January 1951 on a salary of £950 a year.

At first the new works manager found the going tough, with the men not taking kindly to a new arrival who had been given the job many believed should have gone to the acting works manager.

The hostility did not last long, however, and Donaldson found himself in day-to-day control of a brick production plant which was already having to adapt to the boom-slump-boom conditions which were to characterise the construction sector in post-war years.

He became respected and trusted. One pensioner recalls "the Duck," as he became known to the men: "He knew very little about bricks when he arrived but he soon learned. He was an outstanding manager from the workers' point of view. If something was wrong he would put his boiler suit on and work all day Sunday with the men to put it right."

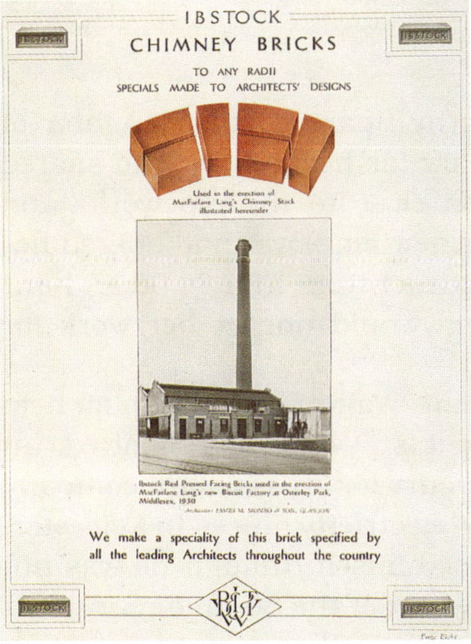

Two pages of a 1930's Ibstock catalogue offering chimney bricks for the modern architect - as used in this Middlesex biscuit factory built for MacFarlane Lang - and bricks for every application, from fireplaces to toy bricks "for happy boys."

Nothing was allowed to hold up the production of bricks, the basic commodity demanded by everyone caught up in the hectic rush to rebuild. They were in desperately short supply and their availability was all that mattered to the customer. Quality often appeared irrelevant and few customers were interested in any variations on a theme. A brick was a brick and it was the responsibility of people like Harry Fyson, the works engineer, to ensure they continued to emerge from the kilns.

Faced by such demand Ibstock was ready by 1954 to invest in a second chamber kiln at the South Works, a development which increased production capacity to 26 million bricks annually. The sales staff was increasingly stretched as it tried to cover the country, clocking up thousands of miles in the search for business.

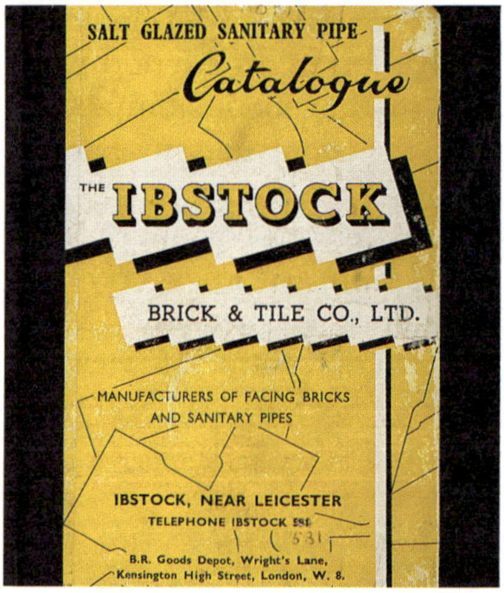

An early Ibstock catalogue offering salt-glazed sanitary pipeware, the production of which did not cease until 1965.

In the Ibstock office Dorothy Sparrow, the daughter of "J.J.", began to work as a secretary for her father, who shared an old office with Jim Donaldson close to the pipeworks and surrounded by mud and dirt. Her new employer had offered her 3s an hour but she managed to extract from him 3s 6d an hour on the grounds that her husband would not let her work for anything less.

It was also in 1954 that John Walton got additional help with the recruitment of Roger List, who had spotted an advertisement in the Leicester Mercury for an assistant company secretary. An accounts clerk in the electricity offices in Leicester, 26-year-old List was keen to better himself, though he was not quite so enthusiastic over the prospect of the 30-mile round trip each day by motorcycle to the Ibstock works.

The salary of £600 a year was enough, however, to persuade him that it was the right decision. On April Fools Day he reported for work at Ibstock's bungalow office where about a dozen people were now employed. Eventually he would take over from Walton as company secretary.

By now Douglas Eves had been called to the Bar and had become deputy chairman, acting - literally - as the chairman's eyes and for a while living in a flat in "Redlands." He admits that, initially, he was more interested in people than in bricks, though his knowledge of the industry inevitably grew as he spent time accompanying the chairman on regular visits to Ibstock.

Jim Donaldson (left) and "J.J." Sparrow ceremoniously lighting up one of the south works kilns.

He recalls fondly the man whose principal desire was to keep the business going so that it could be passed on to the next generation; a man who preferred not to take risks but whose prudent and steady management style had brought the company through challenges which had defeated many of its competitors.

"He was a man of great warmth, marvellous judgement and great patience. He kept dividends low because he always wanted to be in a position to put money back into the business."

But despite Douglas's affection and respect for the chairman and his warmth for the Ibstock workers, he had decided by 1955 that he no longer wanted to stay on. His health had not been helped by his wartime injuries and he was anxious to return to teaching. Ten days before Christmas 1955 the board received his resignation and Paul was at once appointed deputy chairman of Ibstock. His future as a leading figure in the business which had always been a part of his life was now sealed.

Paul left his accountancy practice and joined his father full-time, moving his family from London to Catthorpe in south Leicestershire. Although he by now knew a great deal about the company, his new qualifications enabled him to see Ibstock for what it was - a sound business which commanded amazing loyalties from those who worked within it.

The company was being run tightly, some would claim austerely, a characteristic which was not uncommon among businesses in the locality at that time. There was a popular working philosophy, shared within Ibstock, which decreed that if life was miserable, then things were going well; something was wrong unless work was tolerably uncomfortable.

According to Jim Donaldson: "Everything was run on a shoe-string. You couldn't get anything new in the way of equipment and there were shortages of everything except people who had been displaced by the war. Everyone felt they were underpaid."

It was an approach to work which Paul, who already felt awkward about being the son of the boss, did not relish. Neither was he happy about the tensions he found within the office, with a chain-smoking unrelaxed John Grover always at odds with Jim Donaldson and invariably highly suspicious and openly critical of the new deputy chairman, who had to try and keep the peace.

Paul found an instant ally in "J.J." Sparrow, whose pear-shaped figure and shock of white hair never seemed to be far away when he needed help. He acted as a father-figure to "Mr. Paul," dispensing sound advice based on years of solid experience and demonstrating the skills of gentlemanly management which were to give him a second successful career on the local county council.

The deputy chairman still felt alone, however: "At first it was all pretty depressing. There were few people to confide in and I felt on my own. I was doing the job because I was my father's son but I did not know if I was doing it well or badly.

"As it turned out, it was the best business training I could have had. There was no room for personal pride, which is the last thing you need if you are going to run a business."

As the deputy chairman, in close consultation with his father, began to look towards the future, the final reminders of the company's past were being dismantled.

One of his first tasks was to wind up the last remaining activities of Wellhall Assets which, with Wishaw Coal, had formed part of Dr. Thomson's original business interests in Scotland.

By the 1950's Wellhall existed only in terms of some of the property interests it had acquired in and around Glasgow at the height of its success in the last century. Now, all that remained were rented homes in locations like the infamous Gorbals slums, which had become a liability rather than an asset. Having struggled to try and make the properties offer an economic return, Paul decided to sell the freehold.

A craftsman's touch: tile-making in the 1940's at Warners' Star Works, which Ibstock would buy in 1984.

In April 1957 the directors also accepted a tender of £2,660 for the removal of the Ibstock branch railway and for the scrapping of "Annie," the steam engine which had given such faithful service for more than half a century. By August the junction at Bagworth was removed, thereby severing the brickworks from the national rail network and cutting off the company's historic roots.

There was little time, however, to reminisce. Ibstock could still only claim a very limited range of hand-made and machine-made tapped and sandblasted bricks in colours ranging from red and russet brown to black and silver grey.

In addition there was a range of salt-glazed pipework, manufactured in increasingly inefficient conditions at the rate of 180 tons a week. The company acknowledged that clay pipes faced stiff competition from alternative materials and that its position as a manufacturer of small pipes was becoming "increasingly more uncertain."

But the deputy chairman had been learning fast and, encouraged by some of those around him, began to see the scale of the opportunity which lay in wait for a brick manufacturer with a new approach to his market place.

The brickmakers' approach to selling their product had not, it seemed, changed at all over the years. The product was manufactured and sold directly to merchants, who stocked them in their yards. In turn they sold them on to their own customers.

The identity of the makers of an essentially homogeneous building material was lost or considered irrelevant by its ultimate user.

John Grover - his enthusiasm no doubt fired by excellent commission rates - was already demonstrating that bricks would travel and that the additional costs involved were not a barrier to sales. The proviso was that the architect could see something capable of enhancing his project and that the brick manufacturer could offer a quality product with an equally dependable back-up service.

The sales director's characteristically imaginative approach to selling made the deputy chairman realise that bricks might just be open to promotion in a way which people had previously thought was impossible.

Ibstock began to take a pride in notching up sales around the country, courting the architects and slowly building a sales force which showed an interest in local construction activity and which homed in on prestige projects to convince the specifiers that Ibstock's was the right brick for the job.

The first sales recruit outside London was Graham Walker, who had got to know the brick producers while working for a Watford-based builders merchants. Bored after returning to the same job after completing his national service, Walker saw Leslie Truelove - shortly to be made sales manager - and the deputy chairman. He joined Ibstock in 1959 for £675 a year and a shiny new Morris 1000 Traveller.

He and other newcomers would be sent to the works for a two-month training course, at the end of which they knew more about bricks than they might have imagined was possible. They had to load and unload them, familiarise themselves with the workings of the plant and see the finished product being used on site.

Out on the road Walker and the growing band of representatives - armed with home-made sample racks and a list of fixed prices - each took responsibility for a particular region of the country. So great was the mileage being registered - with 1,000-mile services falling due every 10 days - that an incredulous chairman at first queried the expenses of his sales team.

According to Walker: "We were pioneers, really. We went out to the architects prepared to pay the price, to help on detail and to become part of the team at the earliest stage, maybe nine months before an order would materialise. The others were still relying on builders for their business."

Ibstock was walking a tightrope. The architects were desperately short of bricks and were keen to locate attractive alternatives for a new generation of high-profile projects such as university buildings and local authority headquarters.

But, above all, there was no point in selling the Ibstock name if it could not produce the goods. Paul began to think about a programme of modernisation and expansion which, to many of his colleagues, seemed highly ambitious for a company where growth had been as much by accident as by design.

Douglas Eves, back on the sidelines but still a valued sounding post for Paul, had long and detailed discussions with the deputy chairman about his plans: "The talk was of marketing, rather than producing bricks; about a national brick company. Some of it seemed highly ambitious and possibly more than the company should sensibly tackle. But Paul had an impressive grasp of the detail and convinced people it was the way ahead."

The way ahead meant a new automated brick production facility at the South Works into which the directors decided to inject the company's accumulated funds. It was a radical step and a gamble for a company of such comparatively modest proportions. As one outside observer was to remark later: "They bet the store on the project. If it had failed it might have meant the end of the company."

First Paul had to sell the idea of a "state of the art" plant to his father, who went along with the plan. Work began in 1959 and by the end of 1960 a 20-chamber Staffordshire kiln was ready for commissioning. The new 45,000 sq. ft. unit, all under one enormous roof, cost £270,000 and would be capable of turning out 250,000 bricks a week, boosting the company's annual brick production to 41 million. At the time sales were running at 34 million bricks a year.

The industry was suitably impressed by the towering ambitions of such a modest enterprise. British Clayworker, the industry's trade magazine, said that the construction of large modern brick plants had, because of the pre-requisite for major financial resources, been confined to larger public companies. One noteable exception, it proclaimed, was Ibstock Brick & Tile, which had shown itself capable of defying the tradition.

The new works were opened just before Christmas 1960

when "J.J." Sparrow, now an Alderman, lit the new kiln with a torch which resembled an Olympic flame. Before an audience of businessmen and local civic dignitaries Alderman Sparrow expressed the hope that the bricks produced would be of high quality and low cost. The new plant, he emphasised, could achieve maximum output under the watchful eye of just 26 men.

Despite initial teething troubles the "gamble" paid off and shortly afterwards a fourth kiln was added to the plant, raising Ibstock's annual brick-making capacity to 56 million. In a further break with the past the plant was also switched from coal-firing to oil burning as part of continuing efforts to contain costs and improve reliability.

Paul Hyde-Thomson examines a model of the new South Works which was completed in 1960. The models were built so that his blind father could fully appreciate new developments.

By March 1961 the chairman decided that the time had come to retire from the post. He had few doubts that his son, having clearly demonstrated his management abilities, was more than capable of filling the seat he had occupied for nearly 40 years.

At a board meeting that month the directors praised his "remarkable service" to the company. Among the tributes was one from "J.J." Sparrow, who said the chairman's retirement represented a milestone in the history of a company which was about to be chaired by the fourth generation and fifth member of the same family.

Ibstock, he noted with some pride, had always managed to pay a dividend to its shareholders and it was fitting, in the last year of his chairmanship, that Robert Hyde Hyde-Thomson had been able to preside over a record performance. At the end of the meeting father and son together signed the audited accounts for the last time.

5

Floating bricks

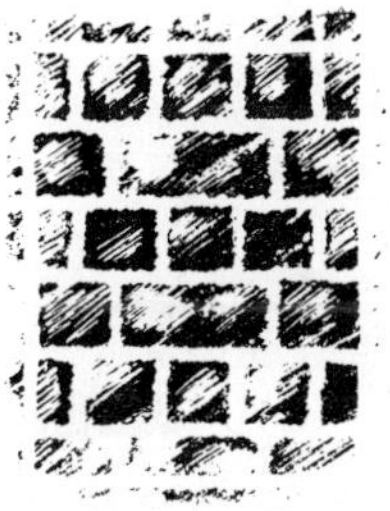

THE new chairman's strategy was working well. Providing the back-up was always reliable and available, Ibstock was beginning to sell increasingly to customers who were looking for somcthing different and who wanted the best. A national market for Ibstock bricks was beginning to emerge.

There were the inevitable complaints over quality and conformity, the chairman being summoned across the country on more than one occasion to explain himself and his bricks to important and angry customers. But the company began to improve margins on its bricks, particularly for its hand-made products.

It was also beginning to make different bricks from different clays, able to offer its customers some variety of product stemming essentially from the differences in techniques which characterised the old and new production plants.

The momentum of success was also making its mark on the rocky relationship between John Grover and Jim Donaldson, who had preferred to sit in their respective rooms and send memos to each other rather than talk. Now they had little time to indulge in office warfare.

Having partially founded its new success on its ability to

offer a variety of bricks, however, the reality was that Ibstock had strictly limited room for manoeuvre. There was only so much a manufacturer could do with Leicestershire clays and, having had their appetite whetted, the building industry wanted a bigger choice.

The marketing penny had dropped and Ibstock began to lead the way for an industry which had never stopped to think about the way it did business.

Robert Hyde Hyde-Thomson presenting "J.J." Sparrow with a gold watch for completing 50 years' service with Ibstock. Mrs Sparrow looks on.

To mark the start of the 1960s the company had invested more than £500,000 on new plant and machinery. Neither had the pipe-making operations been overlooked, with around £160,000 being spent on modernising production facilities so that, if it became profitable, quality clay products other than salt-glazed pipes could be made.

Now the search was on for ways of securing the next stage of the company's expansion and enabling it to offer the wider range of bricks which its customers wanted. The first opportunity to add another quiver to the Ibstock bow was just around the corner.

As Paul's father, now 73, prepared finally to relinquish his directorship - with 82-year old "J.J." Sparrow leaving the board at the same time - the chairman's attention was drawn to a company called Himley Brick, a manufacturer of engineering, common and facing bricks, with good clay reserves estimated to have a life of 100 years, located near Dudley in the Black Country.

Himley had a proud history but faced an uncertain future. The business had been founded in 1847 by Mr. Robert Lucas

Chance to supply refractory bricks to his nearby Glass and Lighthouse Works in Smethwick which had obtained an order to supply one million square feet of glass for the Crystal Palace, built to house the Great Exhibition of 1851.

At the end of the last century the company became the Himley Fire and Red Brick Company. The rich fire clay deposits, which had initially determined the location of the Himley works, enabled mining to continue until the early 1920s. When the workings were eventually flooded the company switched to facing brick production.

Conditions must have been very similar to those at Ibstock. Caleb Bennett was works engineer in the 1920s and recalls the teams of women brick moulders making 900 bricks each a day, placing them on "hot floors" to dry. They worked for less than 10s a week and, at the end of their 10-hour shift, were expected to use the nearby canal to clean up.

"It was not unusual to see the women kneeling on the bank at the end of the day's work, breaking the ice and sweeping aside the odd dead dog or cat, so that they could wash before returning home. Today the working conditions then may appear outrageous but, in fact, Himley employees were better treated

Selling with style - the cover of a Himley Fire and Red Brick Company catalogue proclaiming "The Beauty that is in Bricks."

than most workers and the wages were above average."

Like Ibstock, several generations of the founding family had been responsible for the stewardship of the company up until the 1960s. There were other similarities. The company, which was recording modest pre-tax profits - £66,000 in 1962 compared to £155,000 at Ibstock - had taken a major step in starting to modernise its facing brick facilities with the construction of a new kiln. But it had neither the money nor the confidence to see through its plans.

The logic of a merger was appreciated by both sides and a friendly marriage was arranged after Hyde-Thomson had sought the advice and support of John Keeling at London and Yorkshire Trust, a City issuing house controlled by the Keeling family and known to the chairman since his school days.

At the helm of Himley was Pat Holmes, the 52-year-old managing director who had married into the Chance family but who had no son to succeed him. Holmes, a common-sense manager who knew his bricks, had travelled extensively as a civil engineer and contractors' agent in Mexico, the Sudan and Malaya before joining Himley after the war. He had taken over as managing director from his father-in-law in 1950.

Given Ibstock's additional resources Himley's modernisation could be pursued, thereby expanding the present facing brick output of 15 million a year to 25 million. At the same time common brick production of 14 million a year would be allowed to continue for as long as it remained profitable.

More importantly for Ibstock the acquisition of a business with good deposits of Staffordshire Etruria Marl clay would extend the colours and characteristics of the bricks it could offer its customers and also spread its market base. As an added bonus Hyde-Thomson saw Himley as a partner sharing the same corporate "culture" as his own business.

For Pat Holmes, too, the deal made sense. The company's expansion plans, which were essential if it was to survive, were to demand financial resources which the shareholders were either unable or unwilling to provide. At the same time some of the family were anxious to realise the value of their shareholdings.

The solution for Himley was a merger with Ibstock, which in turn would have to provide a commitment that it would seek a quotation through an early public flotation for some of its shares.

Tony King, Himley's able and bright general manager, who would eventually become Ibstock's deputy chairman, says the courtship was brief: "Some of us knew Ibstock quite well, although they tended to operate in different areas of the market. They went for larger contracts while we produced more expensive products and generally sold in smaller quantities.

"Pat Holmes knew there was no-one following on from the family and that getting the company quoted in a wider vehicle made good sense. To continue with our expansion plans would have required more funds than the family wanted to give. They either had to follow Ibstock's approach and gamble everything, or find someone else to do it."

By the summer the marriage was sealed with an exchange of shares and Holmes joined the Ibstock board, retaining his role as Himley's managing director and becoming director of development for the bigger group. In other boardroom changes to follow John Grover retired early and the hard-working Les Truelove assumed overall responsibility for sales. Jim Donaldson became the company's seventh director.

Now Ibstock's shareholders were informed that, as a result of the merger, producing a combined brick production capacity of 80 million a year, the company would be of a size and status in the industry which made a Stock Exchange quotation both feasible and desirable.

The plan was that, after the share offer, present shareholders would account for 52.5 per cent of the equity, with 22.5 per cent going to Himley shareholders and the remaining 25 per cent being offered to the public.

By the time the share offer package was ready Ibstock was able to report that its merger with Himley was proving successful and that £250,000 had been earmarked for further modernisation programmes at both locations. There were no great changes at Himley, although people like Tony King soon realised that Ibstock's marketing skills were considerably better developed than those of his old employer.

Les Truelove and his team soon got to work to impose the Ibstock sales formula on its new acquisition. "We inherited a small sales staff which was quickly brought into line with our philosophy. There were plenty of initial problems but there was general goodwill and the Himley people seemed happy enough."

Graham Walker, out on the road in his Vauxhall Victor, remembers selling the welcome additions to the company's product line and then wondering how - given some considerable teething problems with Himley's new plant - they were going to be supplied. In the event the problems were resolved and Himley bricks began to enjoy an expanding market.

At the very end of a better-than-expected year for Ibstock, with pre-tax profits of £220,000 confirming the improving profitability record achieved over the previous few years, the offer for sale in the company's shares went ahead.

In the run up to sale day - December 4 - the chairman and his colleagues spent long hours closeted with their financial advisers to ensure the offer went well.

With John Keeling away from his desk at London & Yorkshire, his younger brother Michael found himself deeply involved in the preparations for a critical phase in the development of a company with which he was to remain closely involved. Without him many of Ibstock's future deals would not have been done.

"The chairman was clearly very ambitious to build something big. He was the most amazing client, wanting to understand every single aspect of the offer and proving very demanding in the process."

Shortly before the share sale the company was confronted with a novel choice. Stock Exchange rules had been changed to permit shares to be offered to investors by way of a tender rather than by fixed price.

A strong economy, which was directly reflected in the demand for Ibstock products, meant that the share market was remarkably buoyant and many new issues were running to substantial premiums once quotation began.

During one meeting called to draft the prospectus for the offer Keeling hesitantly raised the possibility that the tender technique might offer the best option for Ibstock. He need not have feared: the chairman had already spotted the opportunity and the company became one of the first to raise cash via a tender offer.

The 612,000 shares were offered at a minimum price of 10s 6d, although another 20,000 were made available to employees at the same fixed price. Les Truelove had been anxious not to see Ibstock workers "scrapping" for them in the open market and pushed successfully for an allocation. The employee's shares were fully subscribed. On the stock market, however, the picture was entirely different, the issue attracting offers ranging from 10s 6d up to 25s. A tender price of 13s was set and the shares were six times over-subscribed. Net proceeds from the share offer amounted to just over £400,000, providing the company with the financial foundations necessary for the next stage in its development. In addition the Ibstock and Himley shareholders had a market for their shares and the company's profile had been significantly heightened.

The director's satisfaction at the success of the venture was, however, to be overshadowed by news of the death - the day before the share offer - of "J.J." Sparrow. The board stood in silence as a tribute to the man who had made such a huge contribution to the company which was now opening a new chapter in its history.

After an exceptionally mild winter, which meant continued high brick sales, Ibstock began 1964 in good shape to capitalise on a thriving market place. In the spring the lease expired on the company's office and depot in Kensington and it broke new ground for the industry with the opening of a showroom in Crawford Street, in London's West End. It was to prove an immediate success and provided a clear, public demonstration of its determination to sell brick like any other product.

The Ibstock board in 1963 shortly after the company was floated. From left to right, David Sheppard, Pat Holmes, Leslie Truelove, Paul Hyde-Thomson, John Walton, Douglas Eves and James Donaldson.

To quote the chairman 1964 - which was to see the election of the first Socialist Government for 13 years - was a "kind year" for brick manufacturers. The volume of orders and inquiries, stimulated by a raft of building incentives, reached unprecedented levels and turnover was to rise by 25 per cent over the previous year.

But the pattern of success was not being repeated by the company's pipe-manufacturing operations. The future of the pipe department had been a matter of increasing concern given the dominance in the market of the larger manufacturers which had invested heavily to make themselves efficient and highly competitive. The introduction of new materials such as pitch fibre and concrete also enabled them to offer a much-extended range of products.

Ibstock was not among them - recording repeatedly poor profits on pipe sales - and it had become increasingly obvious that the company would be unable to keep up with the competition unless it embarked on a similarly extensive investment programme. But the idea seemed out of the question for a business whose future lay primarily in brick production. The directors concluded that the company had no long-term future in the contracting market for second-quality pipes, a decision enforced by the absence of the company's own raw material supplies. The decision was taken to withdraw from the market while the business was still profitable and to replace the pipe works, now producing 9,000 tons a year, with an annual brick-making capacity of around 10 million.

An aerial view of the Ibstock works in 1965 after the completion of a 45,000 sq. ft. extension at the South Works.

A first step was the conversion of the Ooms Ittner kiln - erected many years previously to herald the company's commitment to pipe manufacture - to the burning of bricks. By 1965 the company would withdraw completely from an activity which had accompanied its operations since its earliest days.

In the same year Ibstock's expansion programme was set to take another major stride with the acquisition of a Staffordshire-based brick manufacturer which appeared ripe for plucking.

Pat Holmes was one of the first to spot an opportunity to buy the old-established Aldridge Brick, Tile & Coal Company, located at Aldridge, about 11 miles from Birmingham. He was alerted by a published photograph of the company's board which demonstrated beyond doubt that the business was in the hands of men who had their best years behind them.

It was not only the directors whose longevity was beyond question. Though some of the plant was relatively modern the Arcadia brick production unit, for example, was still driven by a steam-powered beam engine which was destined to end up in the Ironbridge Trust museum.

Tony King, head of the team which would be charged with knocking Aldridge into shape, recalls: "The chairman would occasionally escort people around the works who were interested in industrial archaeology - and I was supposed to make a profit from it." Any new owner would clearly have to embark on a programme of substantial modernisation to get the most from the business.

Like Ibstock, Aldridge's roots had been in coal mining - operating under the Aldridge Colliery Company name until 1930 when the coal became increasingly uneconomic to mine. The Aldridge pit, nicknamed "drybread" by colliery workers who reckoned that was all their wages would buy, finally closed in 1936.

Also like Ibstock the business had been dominated by family interests, most notably the Exleys, who were well-known Shropshire brick and tile makers, and the Adams family, highly respected ironmasters from Wolverhampton. Later Stanley Baldwin, the MP and future Prime Minister, would be an Aldridge shareholder and his son, Earl Baldwin of Bewdley, would serve as a director.

By the time of the name change the company had for years been in the hands of William Clarke, a consulting engineer best known for his work on the Great Western Railway Company, and his son Frederick. Between them, they liquidated the old business and became joint managing directors of the new one.

From then on Aldridge Brick Tile & Coal concentrated on brick production and, by the time Ibstock made its approach, the company operated four plants on one large site, employed 270 people and turned out around 34 million bricks a year.

The business operated through two wholly-owned subsidiaries, Aldridge Brixancole, manufacturing facing bricks, wirecut and pressed engineering bricks and blue bricks, and Aldridge Coal Factors, which operated as a distributor of household coal supplies.

Supporting the business, quite literally, were about 300 acres of land in the Aldridge and Brownhills area, holding valuable reserves of Etruria Marl equivalent to more than 100 years production at the rates of output then in force.

Ibstock's chairman cast his eye over the business and liked what he saw. Aldridge produced good quality facing bricks, had a good local reputation and was was close enough to Ibstock and Himley to make supervision easier.

The death of Aldridge's young general manager, in whom the directors had placed great store for the future, left the company in limbo and ready to talk to potential buyers, a factor which meant an opportunistic Ibstock could not waste any time.

According to Hyde-Thomson: "It was a mouth-watering situation. The business had plenty of cash and no borrowings, and some immensely under-utilised assets. It was barely making profits but, for us, it offered the chance to make major inroads into the west Midlands market. I suppose it was pretty cocky of us to think we could cope but it was an opportunity which seemed too good to miss."

In January 1965 Ibstock made a 30s a share offer for the Aldridge business, valuing it at £700,000. The figure was raised to 32s after further discussions between the two sides. By the end of May the £745,677 bid had been accepted by Aldridge directors and the deal was finalised by the beginning of July.

The chairman told Ibstock shareholders that the company's brick capacity had been raised to 130 million a year and that the Aldridge acquisition would widen the range of brick products, improve the group's competitive abilities and raise trading profits. At the same time Ibstock announced a £400,000 debenture stock issue to help meet the costs of the purchase and of planned modernisation throughout a growing group.

The Aldridge board was reconstituted, leaving only one of the previous directors in place, and work began at once to bring the newly-acquired company, in the words of one executive, "into the 20th Century." Two of the brick plants, including the ancient

Arcadia, would be closed while extra resources would be pumped into those remaining. Jim Donaldson also fought successfully for the construction of a new tunnel kiln.

Ibstock's taste for acquisitions had not been satisfied, however, by the Aldridge deal. By the end of 1965, the company's attention had been drawn by Laing & Cruickshank, its brokers, to a small, facing brick manufacturer owned by Fisons Fertilisers and located near Cambridge.

What made Burwell Brick special was the unique white Gault clay which lay under the fertile Cambridgeshire soil. The resulting bricks were used when architects wanted maximum light reflection and where a permanent smooth white surface was required. Darker and lighter tints were also available and the company produced about 11 million bricks a year.

Fisons was looking for a buyer and Ibstock was looking for ways to raise their market penetration in the eastern half of the country. There were reservations within Ibstock about taking on any more commitments for a while and there was concern also about the age of the plant and the demands it would place on group resources.

Even so, the board eventually proceeded with an offer of £80,000 and the business became part of the group in early 1966. Among the small number of staff who stayed with Burwell under new ownership was Frank Oldroyd, a slightly fussy but well-liked Yorkshireman whose skills were to be put to good use as the company's administrative officer. Many "new boys" had their first impressions of Ibstock formed by the man everyone called "Uncle Frank."

Some of the board's original doubts were eventually to prove justified, however. Burwell was to operate until 1971 when attempts to diversify away from loss-making brick production into land drains also failed. The company's twin 180ft. chimneys - part of the local skyline for many years - were demolished shortly afterwards and the chairman was to admit later that the purchase had been a mistake.

In the meantime Ibstock's thirst for fresh business opportunities had not been quenched. At the end of 1965, for example, it had cast an eye over Roughdale Brickworks, a publicly-quoted facing and common brick manufacturer based at St. Helens in Lancashire. The board decided, however, that involvement would entail heavy financial and management problems and the directors decided to take the matter no further.

Their interest would be reawakened, with more positive results, a few years later.

By the start of 1966, which was to bring much tougher trading conditions, mounting brick stocks and a near-halving of profits, the company was arranging what promised to be its first significant product diversification. In February, as the board paid its respects to John Walton, who died after 44 years with the company and whose position was taken by Roger List, Ibstock was in talks with Shawell Precast Products, a specialist manufacturer of precast cladding.

Shawell, based near Rugby, was a wholly-owned subsidiary of Miller Bros. & Buckley, the construction group. It had only recently been set up in response to the wave of enthusiasm for industrialised buildings which held out the prospect of speedy and profitable construction business.

Although the concept was contrary to Ibstock's philosophy of individuality, the company wanted to popularise the use of brick slips in the make-up of prefabricated slabs, which were invariably made up on site before being lifted into place. At the time everything from marble and brick to granite was being used to face building panels and Ibstock wanted to be able to cash in on the fashion.

Mr Paul Hyde-Thomson, who presided over Ibstock's greatest period of expansion.

A marriage involving its own knowledge of brick and the contracting know-how of a company like Shawell seemed like a sensible way to proceed. It would increase Ibstock's product range and raise Shawell's profitability by extending its market area.

After protracted talks which lasted much of the year a 50-50 partnership deal, costing Ibstock £90,000, was finally struck with Miller Bros. & Buckley in November. Shortly afterwards Leslie Truelove announced he was to retire as sales director because of ill health. He was replaced by Tony King.

The deal with Miller Bros. would eventually lead, in 1970, to full ownership of the associated company. Later the business was put in the hands of Christopher Belk, its general manager, who expressed confidence in the potential for the pre-cast sector. Belk, who went on to become development director of Ibstock Building Products, said the intention was to meet a need which the market clearly wanted fulfilled.

The optimism was to be short-lived. The business operated within the Ibstock camp only until 1977 when, as Ibstock Precast, it was run down after a disappointing history of low volume sales and poor returns.

Only a year before the business was sold off for £1 - the land raised nearly £300,000 - in the shape of a technical licence to Empire Stone of Leicestershire it had announced the end of five years of research and development and put its own brick panels into production. It was too late; the concept had failed to live up to expectations and Ibstock was given a salutary lesson in the benefits of sticking to what it knew best.

6

Mr. Hanson calls

BY the start of 1967, a year in which the market for bricks was set to improve significantly, Ibstock had completed much of the reorganisation and rationalisation needed in the wake of its recent acquisitions. But unforeseen traumas were just around the corner.

A year earlier it had been a company with 10 manufacturing units and a combined annual capacity of 125 million bricks and 10,000 tons of salt glazed pipes. By now, however, there were just six manufacturing plants left with an annual brick capacity of 130 million and employing 14 per cent fewer people.

Fresh emphasis was given to training and management development within a business organisation which now, increasingly, looked less like the Ibstock company of old.

In another sign of changing times, the company confronted a strike. The men charged with packing bricks for transportation to customers walked out, demanding more money for making the switch from straw packaging to paper. Most of the packers withdrew their labour but their resolve collapsed in under a week. The changeover, as it turned out, speeded up the job and actually increased their wages.

The group's spread nationally had taken important strides forward, enabling it to offer a wider range of bricks across a greater number of regions. The sales force was steadily growing, busily trying to woo customers away from local, traditional products with a range of alternatives which took many of them by surprise.

Alan Butler, a regional sales representative at the time, who would eventually become a regional sales manager, remembers the challenging days of "cold-calling."

"You sought out the architects and just knocked on the door, hoping you would get at least a foot in, so that you could introduce yourself and the company. The reaction was often good, as you were offering something new and exciting.

"A lot of time was spent encouraging potential customers to come and look at how we made our bricks. They did not know us or our products but we managed to get many of them on our side by showing them round and letting them see how we operated. It was, and still is, a very beneficial strategy."

Ibstock did not, of course, have the market to itself, with competitors like London Brick - the giant in common bricks - fighting for business in the non-fletton market. Redland, too, was technically adventurous and finding new uses for brick and beginning to appreciate that the commodity it was providing was valued more highly by its customers than the manufacturers themselves had appreciated.

By the summer of 1967, the year in which Jim Donaldson was made production director and given the task of investigating further acquisitions, Ibstock had another name and a new product to add to its expanding interests.

This time the object of its attention was Superbrix, located at Weeford near Tamworth in Staffordshire, which was producing 24 million bricks annually on modern plant and which offered Ibstock the chance to move away from clay and into sand-lime bricks.

The bricks essentially offered a cheaper alternative to their clay counterparts and also provided more scope for the use of different colours. They wore badly, however, and the colours were known to fade. By the time Ibstock became involved Superbrix was in heavy debt to Forward Trust, the hire purchase arm of Midland Bank. Its owners, Ceres Estates, were looking for a way out.

Despite reservations about the advisability of a quality

product company like Ibstock becoming involved in an arguably inferior artificial alternative, Superbrix was purchased for £160,000. The package included some useful tax losses which helped enhance the attractiveness of the deal.

The move was to prove another mistake, however. Ibstock found it hard to achieve sufficiently attractive margins and, four years later, events would take a dramatic turn and help bring to an end another attempt to stray from Ibstock's well-chosen path.

During 1967, which also saw the retirement from the board after 20 years' service of David Sheppard, Ibstock had managed to remain unscathed by the deteriorating economic situation and had notched up profits of approaching £400,000. Along with other facing brick makers it had also escaped from under the cloud of an investigation by the Prices and Incomes Board.

Earlier in the year the Board had permitted an interim price increase of three per cent while it examined the industry's case for larger rises. But by November it had concluded that the ordinary laws of supply and demand could be allowed to apply to the facing brick sector, which it believed should be left free to fix prices at the level it thought the market would bear.

In the immediate future Ibstock was going to need all the help it could get in coping with its first significant recession since its recent expansion. Having performed admirably in 1967, managing to produce a bumper set of results, the company found itself riding the notorious construction "switchback" in the following year. The boom quickly gave way to slump and construction activity, further undermined by an appalling winter, fell sharply.

The weak economic situation had already provoked the devaluation of Sterling, which was to be followed by a gloomy budget and a general slowing in activity. A shortage of funds also saw the building societies having to ration mortgages, making life even harder for the house builder.

With demand for bricks dropping sharply, competition for available business became intense. In a year which brought a rare reverse in Ibstock profits, the company was forced to put more than 15 million bricks into stock. The previous year its increasingly familiar yellow and green vehicles had delivered enough bricks to cut stocks by more than 12 million.

Ibstock was to fare much better than many others, however. With the backing of highly supportive bankers, the company steadfastly maintained its record of steadily rising output, refused to close down any capacity and determined not to resort to cutting its general range of selling prices.

The harder market conditions became, the more effective its aggressive sales pitch became. More than ever Ibstock's sales prowess came to the fore. Sales director Tony King and Graham Walker, who was now group sales manager, were still building a national sales team and paying increasing attention to a London market which had been neglected. Overall, there was now in place a strategy which would come to characterise the company's approach to hard times.

There was also help in the shape of Ibstock's past decision to avoid the public sector housing market, where brick makers began to dump supplies in a bid to notch up sales. Additionally London Brick was forced to embark on a massive reduction in capacity which helped ease the task of other suppliers in winning a share of whatever sales were available.

The Ibstock philosophy was, by now, also hard at work in other directions. The immediate outlook apart, the brick industry was now faced with mounting evidence that it could no longer count on a guaranteed market for its products.

Much of the industry was surviving on minimal profits and competition from other materials. Its difficulties were further exacerbated by the growing success of alternative materials which met Government demands for speedy construction, particularly in respect of high-rise housing. The industry's own morale was low, the outlook was uncertain and, to many people, brick had simply become boring. Its plight was summed up in one, simple statistic; the number of bricklayers employed in Britain had fallen by around one-third in little more than a decade.

A few people remained optimistic, however. During 1968 Sir Ronald Stewart, the chairman of London Brick, had called in the representatives of the larger brick makers - including Paul Hyde-Thomson - to discuss the Brick Development Association's future.

The plan was to transform a production-oriented BDA into a promotion organisation which could help transform what appeared to be an indifferent future for the brick production industry. The Association was reconstituted and, at the beginning of 1969, Ibstock paid £1,000 to join.

The industry appeared, after years of inaction, to be

assuming responsibility for its own future. It was to be the start of a spectacularly successful initiative to drag brick, kicking and screaming, into the second half of the 20th Century. Before 1968 was out Ibstock itself was to confront other pressing challenges of more direct and immediate consequences for its own future.

The chairman's ambitions to expand the business still further had not been dented by the rough going. The year, indeed, was only two months old when he raised with his fellow-directors the possibility of expansion overseas, possibly in Canada, Australia, or even the Caribbean.

Hyde-Thomson was the first to acknowledge the potential difficulties of making such a move, not least in respect of management, but he won the board's approval for his view that it would be better for the company to expand abroad in an industry that it knew well than to diversify at home into products of which it had no knowledge.

By the summer the chairman had pursued the point to the extent of flying to North America to establish the potential for acquisition. He returned, enthused by the scale of the potential market and showing a particular interest in the St. Lawrence Brick Company of Montreal.

The company was operating old and inefficient plant but was not in a position to embark upon an investment programme without the assistance of outside finance. The plan was to make available the necessary working capital in return for which Ibstock would take a controlling interest in the business.

The chairman's excitement at the prospect was not universally shared. Production director Jim Donaldson, who was despatched three times to check out the Montreal operation, was among the sceptics.

Although he saw the potential, Donaldson returned more disillusioned after each visit. He was unconvinced about the extent of the stated clay reserves, unhappy about running a business so far away and was also left with major reservations about the calibre of some of the Canadian company's key personnel.

"I told the chairman he would be wasting the company's money if he decided to go ahead. I thought it would be the biggest mistake Ibstock had ever made and said so. But, each time he went over, he came back more enthusiastic."

The negotiations continued throughout the remainder of the year and, much to Donaldson's relief, the chairman telephoned him on Christmas Eve 1968 to inform him that the deal, after all, was off. It had floundered over terms relating to a long-term loan raised by Ibstock to finance the purchase, although by the end the chairman apparently also shared some of Donaldson's own reservations.

Almost at once Ibstock found the tables turned with two companies expressing an interest in its own activities. Both were furnished with the information necessary to consider making a bid. Although one, a West Midlands-based property and construction business called Lunt Comley & Pitt, did not take the idea any further, it became clear that the other was intent upon doing a deal.

The business in question was the Wiles Group, a small industrial holding operation run by Mr. James Hanson. Based in Hull, it had won a stock market flotation in 1964 and, although still heavily dependent for its livelihood on commercial vehicle distribution, it was firmly set upon expansion and diversification.

A quarter of century later Hanson would have become Britain's leading corporate acquisitor capable of mounting cash bids worth billions of pounds for businesses he wanted brought under his world-wide umbrella.

At the end of 1968, however, it was merely a small business with big ambitions. Based in Pont Street, London SW, behind Harrods, Wiles' small management team had been researching the industries which it believed were worthy of further interest.

Despite the apparently bleak prospects for brick, Wiles was attracted to the industry, given the company's knowledge of transport and its record in operating local autonomous businesses which required considerable on-the-spot entrepreneurial flair.

Earlier the same year it had sought and acquired Butterley Brick, another facing brick specialist, whose availability on the market had also aroused the interest of the the Ibstock directors. Although the sale to Wiles had been quickly wrapped up Ibstock wondered whether Butterley's new owner might consider selling on. By January 1969, however, Hyde-Thomson was telling his directors that Wiles was preparing a bid for their own business.

In the first week of February, as the two sides talked about the possibility of a Wiles takeover, a large buying order for Ibstock shares, placed through a Swiss bank, alerted the stock market that something was up. An announcement was hurriedly issued to the press, revealing that discussions which could lead to an offer for Ibstock were underway. The company emphasised it would not be prepared to recommend any deal which did not value the shares at "significantly above" 22s 6d each. On the day in question Ibstock shares raced up by over 4s to close at 18s 6d.

By the middle of February, as Douglas Eves announced his resignation from the board after 22 years' service, the details of an agreed takeover had been formulated in a series of meetings involving Hyde-Thomson, Michael Keeling, James Hanson, Gordon White, his associate, and Derek Rosling, the company secretary.

The deal was based on an offer of 27s 3d a share which the Ibstock board said it could recommend and which it intended to accept in respect of the shareholdings it represented, amounting to 20 per cent of the ordinary share capital. Together with other pro-takeover shareholdings, more than one-third of the equity was happy with an offer which valued Ibstock at £3.6m.

Details of the bid, which was conditional upon Wiles being satisfied that Ibstock's publicly-stated profit forecast of £400,000 for 1969 was achievable, were despatched on February 14. One week later, Wiles withdrew its offer.

Hanson had come to the conclusion that, after a quick but detailed investigation, Ibstock's forecasts for sales and profits were doubtful. With the financial year so young Wiles concluded that detailed figures were impossible to calculate and there were sufficient reservations to stop the agreement in its tracks.

A form of words was agreed between the two companies and on February 21 the City was informed that the takeover had been abandoned. There was considerable embarrassment within Ibstock, which felt that it had emerged badly from the episode.

Derek Rosling, who was to become vice-chairman of Hanson, says the Wiles team was stoical about its failure to pick up another brick producer: "We were still learning and the temporary set-back can hardly be said to have put us off our stride."

In the event Wiles' doubts about the sales and profit forecasts, in what turned out to be a very tough year for the industry, were fully justified. Works closures among brick makers were announced almost daily, with national sales falling by over 10 per cent and brick stocks reaching more than one billion for the first time. As a result Ibstock profits in 1969 reached only £293,000.

According to Ibstock's chairman: "Mike Keeling was away at a crucial period in our discussions, which did not help and we came out of the whole chapter looking bad.

"The whole thing was very quick and we were no match for James and Gordon. They were very clever operators and extremely impressive, although we had little in common personally."

Within weeks of the collapse of the deal Michael Keeling joined the Ibstock board. One fellow director was so impressed with the Wiles operation that, soon after the dust had settled, he took it upon himself to buy shares in Hanson's business.

A little later in 1969 Wiles changed its name to Hanson Trust and began to grow in a way which would turn the business into an international corporate giant large enough to rank alongside the world's most impressive corporate empires. Within a very short time it would again cross Ibstock's path.

7

An odd marriage

HOW much Ibstock's public rejection by Wiles shaped its attitude to its own future remains a matter for conjecture but it is certainly true that, from 1970 onwards, the company's development assumed a fresh momentum and there was a new confidence in its ability to remain independent. The year 1970 was itself to prove critically important for Ibstock, embracing as it did its full quota of corporate dramas and personal sadnesses.

In a year of changes the first occurred on January 1, when brick makers switched to metric sizes. Ibstock, not unnaturally, had been among the leaders within the sector in converting to the new dimensions, which it succeeded in doing without having to pass on to its customers any of the costs incurred.

A week later, however, the company looked briefly to its past with the announcement of the death of Robert Hyde Hyde-Thomson, its previous chairman and the man who had sensitively steered the business through its transition from a mining company to a brick producer.

His life was rightly portrayed as a triumph of will over terrible disability while his astute, gentlemanly approach to business established a pattern of excellence which was to become an Ibstock hallmark. That the business should come to be dubbed by the press the "Rolls Royce" of brick producers was in no small way a result of his half-century of endeavour.

Within weeks of Robert Hyde Hyde-Thomson's death Ibstock was considering its next corporate step, based on the conversion of a life-long friendship into a mutually beneficial business partnership.

Since his national service days Ibstock's chairman had enjoyed a friendship with Richard Johnsen who, with his brothers Roy and Peter, had followed in the footsteps of their father to run Johnsen, Jorgensen and Wettre, a privately-owned, international wood pulp agency. Its roots went back to the first years of the 20th Century when it emerged as an independent business from Johnsen and Jorgensen, a Norwegian-based family company which was later to grow separately into a diverse international business group.

During the 1960s the friendship had also developed into an informal business relationship, with Paul Hyde-Thomson employing his accounting skills to provide financial advice to the Johnsen brothers. By the time talk of merger between the two sides was in the air JJW had itself built up a near-15 per cent stake in Ibstock, making it the brickmaker's largest shareholder.

JJW acted as agent for about one dozen hard and softwood pulp mills around the world, arranging sales to paper mills predominantly in the United Kingdom but also to buyers in countries like Australia and South Africa.

JJW's interests extended to a stake in International Fibre Sales, a Geneva-based wood pulp agency, and it also owned Montreal-based Gravetye Sales, which had been set up to sell British papermaking machinery to the Canadian pulp and paper industry but which had ended up selling North American wood pulp to other Commonwealth countries.

The business also held an increasingly valuable 15 per cent share stake in Eucalyptus Pulp Mills, a publicly-quoted holding company which, in turn, owned the Companhia de Celulose do Caima mills and plantations operation in Portugal. The Caima plant in the north, together with a newer mill on the River Tagus at Constancia, manufactured sulphite pulp from eucalyptus wood which the company also grew and which was used in the production of high-grade paper.

JJW was, in short, a commission-based cash-rich company whose "goodwill" balance sheet contrasted with the asset-rich profile of Ibstock. But its 50 or so principal shareholders were locked into an investment which they were largely unable to realise.

Ibstock, on the other hand, was short of the funds required to finance the further expansion which would spread its traditional marketing area. It was also keen to reduce its vulnerability to the cyclical nature of the brick industry. Knowing JJW well it did not envisage any problems in a working relationship which, it readily acknowledged, might be regarded as somewhat strange by industry observers.

Major Roy Johnsen, who joined the Ibstock board in 1970 when the present company was formed by the merger of Ibstock Brick & Tile Co. and Johnsen, Jorgensen & Wettre.

Peter Johnsen recalls a weekend in 1969 when the Hyde-Thomsons came to stay with his family. While out on a walk he raised the subject of a merger, emphasising JJW's resources and Ibstock's plans for growth. "Why don't we get together," he inquired?

Paul promised to mull it over, although his immediate and understandable reaction was to predict bemusement in the City at such a proposal. Despite his reservations, however, talks aimed at reaching an agreement between two companies of roughly equal value got underway as the year progressed.

It was eventually agreed that the initial capital of Ibstock Johnsen, the new holding company, would be £1.5m, divided approximately 53 per cent to former Ibstock shareholders and 47 per cent to those with shares in JJW.

According to Peter Johnsen: "To us, the deal seemed entirely natural. We had around £1m burning a hole in our pocket and Paul clearly had plans which would put it to very good use. We produced cash and the brick business was always cash-hungry. We also felt we were becoming a bit too dependent on one activity and so some element of diversification made good sense from our point of view as well."

Richard Johnsen says that JJW's staff, which numbered around 30 and were based in London's Old Bailey, had no difficulty in understanding the logic of the move. "The task was a little harder when it came to explaining to others in the pulp industry. But it was predominantly a financial arrangement which resolved problems for both of us."

For Paul Hyde-Thomson the advantages were clear: "We wanted to break out of the Midlands and into other regions but we did not have a stash of money to help us on our way.

"We were managing the recession better than most and had not been forced to batten down the hatches. In fact, we were doing comparatively well and thought we had better take advantage of it.

"The deal with JJW, which seemed like a mini-banking operation given the flow of money coming through in commissions, offered an instant release of money for us and a share quote for the Johnsens.

"I had immense difficulty in explaining to the City the financial, rather than the commercial, logic of the arrangement. As an added bonus, it brought new blood to the board and a fresh mix of ideas."

Given the differing activities virtually no integration became necessary apart from at board level, with directors from both companies joining the board of Ibstock Johnsen when the new group was incorporated in July 1970.

Ibstock Johnsen won its new stock exchange quotation in November of the same year. Both companies were also represented on the boards of Johnsen, Jorgensen and Wettre and Ibstock Brick & Tile, the two operating subsidiaries. From the time of the merger the two businesses have retained their autonomy in a working relationship which has confirmed the strategy behind the original deal and confounded the critics.

The merger was to prove highly astute and very well-timed. As the chairman would put it later: "It gave us the ammunition to go hunting." The group's second wave of growth was just around the corner, waiting for the country to emerge from the recession.

Even as the ink on the JJW-Ibstock agreement was drying, Hyde-Thomson was launching a board-level debate on the new group's expansion strategy. A host of potential targets were named, including Butterley, the Hanson-owned brickmaking subsidiary, National Star Brick and Tile of Newport, Monmouthshire and a number of factories owned either by the National Coal Board or the British Steel Corporation.

One company in particular, however, had attracted the chairman's renewed interest. It was Roughdales Brickworks, the St. Helens-based brickmaker over which Ibstock had cast an eye five years previously.

The business had its own long history, with evidence that bricks had been made at one of its plants in the early part of the 18th Century. But like Ibstock, Roughdales had originally made its money from coal extraction - some local workings dated back to the 16th Century - and had only turned away from coal mining to rely entirely on bricks after the General Strike.

Having shut down its old labour-intensive brickworks, the company now boasted two of the most up-to-date brick making units in the country and was producing around 40 million facing bricks a year - including some hand-made and special shapes - between its Eltonhead and nearby Chester Lane plants. Included was its well-known "Kurtz" range, named after the proprietor of one of St. Helen's original brickworks.

Roughdales's plans for further modernisation had been hit by the recession and there was a deep boardroom split over the best way ahead for the business. The company had also been in trouble because it had sacrificed much of its customer goodwill with an inefficient and unresponsive sales strategy.

The Lancashire company had, in short, experienced something of a chequered history in the previous few years. To add to its problems there had been repeated changes of personnel at director and senior management level.

Hyde-Thomson believed that there were no problems new management could not resolve and Roughdales represented an acquisition opportunity which he and his colleagues were determined not to miss. For Ibstock Roughdales offered not only an extended product range but an important and new regional market.

The two companies, on this occasion, were brought together by nothing more than coincidence. Hyde-Thomson had gone to see Slaughter & May, the solicitors, to discuss the affairs of a family trust and found himself talking to Nigel Harris, who had been put into Roughdales as a "company doctor" chairman to try and sort out the business and its battling directors.

By November 1970 the two sides were exchanging information in preparation for a likely bid. Later the same month, however, Ibstock's board was informed that another of its "target" companies was on the receiving end of a takeover bid.

The company was National Star Brick and Tile and the predator was none other than James Hanson. It was not the first time that National Star had been approached by Hanson but each time it had politely shown him the door. On this occasion, however, the board was merely non-commital on first receiving the terms of Hanson's £800,000 loan stock bid. It was a measure of Hanson's determination to win that it foiled a national postal stoppage by delivering its offer documents by hand to around 2,000 National Star shareholders. Less than a dozen failed to receive the bid terms.

The attraction for Hanson was the location of National Star, whose principal market area lay alongside that of Butterley Brick, the Hanson subsidiary. Butterley already had some large customers in Wales, which it was serving from its Derbyshire plant, and a merger would enable it to cover the Welsh market from National's units in the principality.

But if National Star and its annual output of 90 million bricks had its attractions for Hanson, then the same went for Ibstock. With a production plant at Heather, close to Ibstock, and other factories in Wales, the National Star operation would fit nicely into Ibstock's expansion plans.

The amalgamation of the two businesses would create a group with a production capacity in excess of 220 million bricks a year, capable of withstanding the pressure of competition and offering considerable scope for rationalising sales and distribution networks.

Hyde-Thomson sought an early meeting with National Star to see if Ibstock could improve on what, according to the Financial Times, was Hanson's "generous" offer.

National Star saw the bid in a somewhat different light. A week before Christmas a statement called Hanson's offer "inadequate, unsatisfactory and unfair." The company, which had a patchy record of profits and losses, expressed its faith in a full recovery and an independent future.

Four days later Ibstock entered its first contested takeover bid, valuing National Star at £900,000. There was no response until the first week of the New Year, by which time the Hanson bid had lapsed, its chairman saying only that it would watch with interest the next steps in the saga.

National Star's response to Ibstock was outright rejection, based largely on the grounds that its own shareholders would end up with only a small stake in the enlarged company.

In mid-January Hanson struck again, revealing a new bid worth £1.17m to reflect the potential for increased profits for National Star in 1971. The pursuit hotted up. Four days later Ibstock topped the Hanson offer with a 16s per share bid valuing National Star at £1.25 and winning the support of the directors. But a further, final bid from Hanson raised the value of National Star to £1.39m. It was enough to win the day, with Ibstock refusing to go further and National Star, for the first time, recommending acceptance of a Hanson package.

Ibstock's attention refocussed on Roughdales, which was by now being tipped in the press as an obvious takeover target. On this occasion, however, Ibstock saw to it that there were to be no other intruders. According to Hyde-Thomson: "We rushed into completing the deal. People were taken into rooms and no-one was allowed to leave until everyone had signed."

On March 23 - the day after Paul Hyde-Thomson handed over his responsibilities as managing director of Ibstock Brick & Tile to Tony King - Ibstock announced an agreed £865,000 bid for the St. Helens business. Another important piece in Ibstock's national marketing patchwork had been stitched into place. Graham Walker, in his first week as group sales director, was told by his chairman: "Now you have the output of two more factories to sell."

Despite the flurry of activity intended to strengthen Ibstock's own business prospects, the chairman had also been spending time on efforts to establish some form of industry-wide initiative aimed at improving the outlook for the brick industry.

For much of the post-war period the fletton and non-fletton brick sectors had kept themselves at arms' length, fighting each other for customers. Fletton had been expanding its market share at the expense of the facing manufacturers but, gradually, both sides had come to realise that the real threat to their future lay not in the other but in the shape of competition from other materials such as steel and glass and, particularly, concrete.

Through much of the previous two decades the rush to build had given concrete an unprecedented popularity, at least among designers if not the general public. It was a fashion which drew extreme reactions from traditionalists, some of whom were exercised enough to form a group called the "anti-uglies" who marched against what they saw as the desecration of Britain's "street-scapes" by overbearing monuments to industrialised building methods.

Their anger was directed at the architects responsible, who were even accused of wearing corduroy trousers because they were the nearest thing to the cloth equivalent of corrugated concrete. The slump in brick sales had again served to underline the industry's vulnerability to economic cycles and painfully highlighted its continuing inability to promote itself more positively.

Towards the end of 1970 Hyde-Thomson's frustration at the lack of progress being made by the Brick Development Association had prompted him to give notice of Ibstock's intention to leave the Association if positive results were not forthcoming.

The threat appeared to work. By the start of 1971, in which demand for bricks was to soar and stockpiles would melt away, the Association decided to seek a director general and some high-calibre executive officers to spearhead a promotional drive for an industry which appeared to have lost its confidence and its way.

The Association's new-found resolve led to the appointment of Tony Cadman, a man whose marketing teeth had been cut in the US and who impressed the BDA with his knowledge and his irrepressible enthusiasm for the job. Cadman was to pick up the brick industry by its ears and shake it until it paid attention. His appointment was a gamble and was to prove highly controversial but, in the final analysis, it achieved the desired effect.

As Cadman recalls: "By the time I arrived, the brick industry had a turnover of nearly £130m a year and was recording virtually no profits. It had suffered at the hands of competitive materials, appeared to have lost faith in itself and was in a spiral of decline."

In Cadman's opinion Ibstock was about the only brick company which began to understand marketing: "It was way ahead of the others. It was already packaging its bricks, for example, when most were content to dump them loose on site, with all the consequent damage and loss. The concept of design centres for brick was a measure of the company's farsightedness."

It certainly seemed that few champions of brick were left. The exceptions were people like Jack Milsted, then BDA chairman, Jeremy Rowe of London Brick, Geoffrey Armitage from George Armitage, Maurice Whitehouse of Sussex and Dorking Brick, David Jones of Sevenoaks Brick and Paul Hyde-Thomson.

His first task was to compile a report on the state of the industry, which would carry a blunt message. "I told the industry it had to turn itself on its head and stop seeing itself as the manufacturer of a basic commodity but the producer and promoter of the best building material of them all; one which had endless, artistic applications and which was environmentally attractive." It was a message which a few already understood and which had to be communicated to the rest of the industry.

As Tony Cadman embarked on his crusade Ibstock returned to the hunt for other brickmakers which might join an expanding stable of high-quality production centres that appeared to be more successful the more they retained their autonomy.

Though there were by now uniform reporting and accounting systems within Ibstock, they were not centralised. Separate profit centres were not, the company found, inconsistent with the establishment of a national production and sales network.

Even with its recent growth Ibstock still only commanded about three per cent of the brick market in terms of units of output. With approximately 300 smaller businesses still operational, the shopping list remained a lengthy one.

By the summer of 1971 another name headed Ibstock's list. It was that of the Midland Brick Company, which was owned by the National Coal Board and which had a number of plants at locations like Cannock, Hednesford, Desford and Whitwick.

Earlier in the year Ibstock had received a letter from Lord Robens, the NCB chairman, saying he would be prepared to negotiate the sale of the Board's brickmaking activities to the highest bidder. Its brick interests extended beyond Midland Brick, with an annual output of 70 million, to the Northern Brick Company, where output was running at 80 million annually, and to the Whittlesea Brick Company, producing another 120 million bricks a year. In all the NCB owned 46 separate brick plants, all of which had been inherited from the private sector on nationalisation of the coal industry. For Ibstock, however, the jewel in the crown was the 40-acre NCB plant at Desford just to the south of Ibstock itself. The unit comprised an old and a new production plant, together producing just under 42 million non-fletton bricks annually. In addition there were 40 acres of clay reserves.

The two sides began protracted and complicated negotiations at the NCB's headquarters at Hobart House in London. Despite its original readiness to sell off its brickmaking assets in whole or in part, the Board soon made it clear that any break-up would be confined to selling separately the two principal businesses.

By the end of the year, however, after months of haggling, heads of agreement had been drawn up for the sale of Desford to Ibstock for £600,000. As part of the package Ibstock had also to agree to lease other brickmaking units within the company.

While the negotiations continued Ibstock had successfully completed talks to purchase the remaining half-share in the Shawell concrete cladding business, which was still struggling to make its mark. The company eventually would be renamed Ibstock Precast and, despite optimistic noises about its prospects, it would fail and face gradual wind-up in 1977-8.

More immediately Ibstock as a group was thriving as its talks with the NCB dragged on. There was good weather, interest rates fell, private house-building surged ahead and the business was to notch up its first £1m annual profit. Over the year, during which it began converting many of its kilns to natural gas, it would despatch a record 185 million bricks to its growing list of customers. But in July, shortly after the retirement of Pat Holmes as Ibstock's controller of development and managing director of Himley, the company was to be brought up in its tracks by an appalling accident.

On the last night of the month and at the height of a dramatic storm, a steam-pressurised autoclave used for baking bricks exploded at the Superbrix plant at Weeford. The explosion wreaked havoc around the works, sending parts of the 74ft.-long pressurised vessel more than 200ft. into a nearby wood. When the rubble was cleared one night-shift worker was found dead and another colleague had been injured.

The disaster, which was ascribed to failure correctly to close one of the autoclave doors, led directly to the closure of the Weeford business just at a time when it was becoming profitable.

Express & Star

WALSALL

ASSOCIATED WITH SHROPSHIRE STAR

Wolverhampton Phones: News Desk 22351; Want Ads 27878 — Saturday, July 31, 1971 — No. 30019 PRICE 2½p

Man killed in explosion, family made homeless

DEATH STORM HITS MIDLANDS

● The wrecked brickworks at Weeford, near Lichfield, after the explosion and fire.

The house at Haughton, near Stafford, which was struck by lightning.

A severe thunderstorm brought death and destruction to the West Midlands early today. A Lichfield man was killed and a colleague seriously hurt in an explosion, and a family was made homeless after a thunderbolt ripped through their house.

The Lichfield men, who were due to start their holidays today, were working in a brickworks near Weeford when the blast wrecked the buildings.

It is believed that lightning could have caused the explosion at the brickworks of Aldridge Brixancole, Ltd.

Police said the dead man was Mr. Douglas Leach, believed to be aged about 40, of Pipers-croft, Lichfield. His body was found amongst the debris of the building.

The other man is Mr. William Smith, aged about 24, of Friday-acre, Lichfield. He is in Good Hope Hospital, Sutton Coldfield, with burns to his face and arms.

SHATTERED

The blast, just after midnight, ripped off the asbestos roof building where the bricks are cured in a pressure vessel.

A large hole was blown in the side of the building and windows over a wide area were shattered.

Firemen from Lichfield and Tamworth searched through the rubble after it was thought one of the men were trapped.

A television set was blown apart and severe damage caused to the roof and brickwork of a Streetly house when lightning struck.

Mr. Stephen Nunns and his wife were in bed asleep at 2, Linforth-drive when the house was struck. They were unhurt.

Turn to back page

Test boot for Snow

Sussex fast bowler John Snow, the scourge of the Aussies on last winter's Ashes-winning tour, has been dropped by England selectors for disciplinary reasons.

This is the sequel to an incident involving Snow and Indian opening batsman, Sunil Gavaskar, on the final day of the first Test at Lord's on Tuesday.

Gavaskar and Snow collided as the Indian was running a single and the England star appeared to barge him. When Gavasker fell to the ground and lost his hold of his bat, Snow picked it up and threw it to him.

He was later instructed to apologise to Gavaskar, which he did, but the England selectors obviously felt the matter should not be allowed to rest at that.

Confirming that Snow had been disciplined, the chairman of the selectors, Alec Bedser, said: "My committee and I intend to ensure to the best of our ability that the game of cricket is conducted at all times in the right manner."

Snow had only just returned to the side after missing the series against Pakistan.

His place in the 12 for the second Test at Old Trafford, which starts on Thursday, is taken by Lancashire's Peter Lever.

(Full story—back page)

Spacemen fix oxygen leak

Astronauts David Scott and James Irwin, awakened early today after an oxygen leak developed in the descent stage of the Falcon lunar lander, quickly found the trouble and corrected it. Working on instructions from Mission Control at Houston, the pair located the problem as an open dump valve of the urine receptacle.

Scott and Irwin, who woke an hour early because of the fault, decided not to go back to sleep but said they would use the extra time to get "squared away" for their first Moon buggy ride later today.

The slow oxygen leak created a brief emergency.

After the leak had been stopped, mission control told Scott: "It looks like we can tell you that at the present time we will have sufficient oxygen for a purely nominal (normal) mission."

The oxygen supply is also designed to recharge the portable life-support systems for the astronauts' space-suits on the third of their planned lunar explorations.

"It looks like we will meet that, although rather closely," the Houston control centre added.

Scott responded: "Okay, we will breathe slowly and save as much as we can."

The Apollo 15 crew set up Moon base last night after a perfect descent from orbit.

Directors face cash charges

Three men appeared in court at Bow-street, London, today accused of demanding 18,000 dollars with menaces from a London charter flight company chief.

They were all remanded in custody until Wednesday after Detective - sergeant Michael Keenan had objected to bail.

The men are Ronie Polacco (36), travel agent, of the Londonderry House Hotel, Park-lane, Oswald le Winter (40), company director, and art director Bernard Weil (40), both of Kensington-close Hotel, Wrights-lane, Kensington.

The three, all said to live in America, were charged with demanding money with menaces from director of Expo International Charter Flight Consultants on Friday.

Holiday delayed

A party of Midland holidaymakers bound for Spain were delayed for over five hours at Birmingham Airport today.

They were booked on a Channel Airways flight due to leave for Gerona on the Costa Brava at 9.30 a.m.

The holidaymakers were booked with Lyons Tours, Ltd., Colne, Lancashire.

Trouble as fans march on town

Many Manchester United fans marched 30 miles over the Pennine moors during the night for today's Watney Cup match with Halifax Town.

And before the game started gangs roamed the streets and smashed public house windows. Several thefts from shops were reported.

One store had to close for a while to tidy up after a gang of 200 had marched through, setting off the fire alarm and overturning displays.

Police said that five arrests had been made by lunchtime on charges of disorderly behaviour and theft.

● United's ground has been closed for a fortnight at the start of the Football League season because of a knife-throwing incident.

Soldiers jailed

SAIGON. — Ten former South Vietnamese soldiers have been given jail sentences ranging from six to 18 months for their part in a gun battle with police after a dispute over ex-soldiers' housing and pensions.

Front-page disaster! The Weeford explosion hits the headlines.

The directors were told by Tony King that around £100,000 would be needed to restore Weeford to working order, a level of investment which could not be justified by the returns achieved. Ibstock's efforts in the calcium silicate brick market were at an end.

The end of 1971 found Ibstock preparing to assimilate the plant and personnel of Midland Brick with high hopes that contracts would be exchanged before December was out. But just before Christmas, the NCB found itself in pay negotiations with the miners and it feared that any public announcement about the intended sale of Coal Board assets could upset an already delicate situation.

Nevertheless the Board gave Ibstock an assurance that the agreement would be signed by the end of January 1972. Despite suggestions in the press that the Labour Party was threatening to re-nationalise without compensation any part of the coal industry that was hived off, Ibstock remained resolute in its objective. Even so, the chairman reported that he intended to inquire into the possibility of insuring against any such subsequent occurrence.

In the event the prospect of re-nationalisation was to prove of no consequence. By the middle of January, with the NCB confronting a strike by the country's miners, it informed Ibstock that the deal was off. The political situation had made it impossible.

Ibstock greeted the decision with a mixture of deep disappointment and, after the prolonged uncertainty, some relief. There was some hope that, once the strike was resolved, the sale could be resumed. Indeed the brick plants were eventually put back on the market and Midland Brick eventually found itself in the Hanson Trust stable.

It did not take Ibstock long to bounce back from its disappointment and 1972 was to see another clutch of acquisitions as the group responded positively to a period of mounting profitability which began to make available funds for further investment.

Ibstock's hunger for new acquisitions appeared voracious. As one enthusiastic newspaper share tipster put it: "There is still a tremendous impetus behind the group. Unlike some of its competitors, it is not simply sitting back, waiting for the world to come knocking on its door. It is out there, looking for new customers and more companies."

Within a few months the group scanned a number of potential takeover targets. One successful foray involved North Eastern Bricks, a small producer four miles from the centre of Newcastle - an area the company was keen to penetrate - and based on 90 acres of clay-bearing land which was leased from the Church Commissioners. Instead of being wound up, it joined Ibstock with a price tag of £85,000. The new owners at once prepared modernisation and expansion plans.

The group was to have less luck with another privately-owned company by the name of Lumley Brick, which produced an attractive range of coloured facing bricks from two plants near Sunderland. Ibstock had not figured on the redoubtable figure of Lady Serena James, the chairman and the largest shareholder. Unlike some of her fellow shareholders she was not over-enamoured by the Ibstock offer and refused to sell.

There were, in any case, bigger fish to fry. Once more with its sights on the north, Ibstock's attention had alighted on Nostell Brick & Tile, courtesy of London & Yorkshire Trust, which had been brought in to advise on the financing of a £250,000 modernisation programme.

An early drawing of the Cattybrook works near Pilning, Almondsbury.

Nostell, situated near Wakefield, was producing around 14 million bricks annually from clay which Ibstock believed was capable of yielding high quality facing bricks. The works were on a nine-acre freehold site, although the quarry itself was leased from Lord St. Oswald at the sum of 2s per thousand bricks produced.

Ibstock was prepared to pay £200,000 for the business, which slotted perfectly into its geographic jigsaw, but Nostell held out for £250,000. By the end of May the deal was sealed for £225,000 cash and the new owners prepared to invest well over £1m in order to boost production.

While the Nostell agreement was being hammered out

Ibstock was simultaneously securing the ownership of another strategically-located brickmaker, this time near Bristol in the south west.

The Cattybrook Brick Company stood on good freehold land near to Almondsbury and operated three aging Guthrie kilns which were in need of significant capital investment. Its product range, according to Ibstock, was "most attractive." There was also the unused Shortwood plant at nearby Mangotsfield in the parish of Pucklechurch. It stood silent on 130 acres of land which Ibstock realised could easily accommodate a new production unit.

Cattybrook, like the company which now showed an interest in it, had a long and proud history. It had been established in 1865 by Charles Richardson who, at one stage, served as an assistant to Isambard Kingdom Brunel, the celebrated engineer.

Mr. Charles Richardson, the founder in 1865 of the Cattybrook Brick Company which Ibstock acquired in 1972.

A shrewd, civil engineer with mutton-chop whiskers who recognised that the industrial growth of south Wales could demand a direct railway link with England, he drew up plans for a tunnel under the River Severn. A site was chosen at New Passage and work began in 1858 on what was to become known as the Patchway Tunnel.

While supervising construction the engineer in Richardson noticed that the clay being extracted appeared to be extremely suitable for the production of high-quality engineering bricks. He investigated further, leased a few acres of land and went ahead with the construction of a small primitive

The Bristol headquarters of The Imperial Tobacco Company, built with Cattybrook brick. Designed in 1884, it was refurbished in the 1980s, also using Cattybrook brick.

brickworks.

The resulting bricks were hard and colourful, and superior to anything which could be found at that time in the West Country. They sold well immediately. With no skilled craftsmen in the area, brickmakers were brought in from Nottingham and housed in a row of cottages built especially for them.

Richardson was subsequently employed as chief engineer for the construction of the Severn Tunnel, into which no fewer than 30 million of his bricks were incorporated. By 1875 Richardson had teamed up with Mr. Ernest Street, one of his younger assistants, and Cattybrook Brick was created.

As with Ibstock the company was to be run by a family dynasty, with successive generations of Richardsons at the helm until Ibstock's arrival on the scene.

The company developed during the early part of the 20th Century, building a narrow gauge railway to bring clay from the pit to the works. It gradually extended its product range to embrace a wide variety of red, gold and grey rustic and smooth-faced bricks, together with the "specials" which have become a Cattybrook hallmark and the red terracotta products which still embellish many buildings in the Bristol area.

Brothers Peter (left) and Richard Johnsen, who became directors in the 1970s. They came into Ibstock's life after their family company, Johnsen, Jorgensen and Wettre, merged with Ibstock Brick & Tile Co to form Ibstock Johnsen.

To Ibstock the business represented a golden opportunity. Cattybrook's reputation was high, though its plant was badly out of date; the geographical location was perfect, offering an opportunity to extend Ibstock's penetration of important markets in the south west and south Wales.

Talks aimed at reaching agreement on the terms of the acquisition were amicable and speedy. Tony King, who was involved in the negotiations, recalls holding secret discussions in the office of J. A. Seymour Williams, the Cattybrook chairman and also the coroner for Bristol. Dressed in his beagling clothes he would arrive direct from presiding over an inquest. One day after lunch the negotiators were even invited to view the bodies.

By the end of June 1972 the sale was completed at a cost to Ibstock of £500,000. It at once embarked on plans to install new plant which, at a cost of nearly £1m, would raise output from 11 million bricks to 25 million bricks a year.

In the same year Ibstock streamlined the brick division's structure, merging the growing number of subsidiaries with their parent companies and promoting group identity by ensuring that the Ibstock name figured prominently in each operation.

Graham Walker was directing the company's marketing thrust from Ibstock, expanding and gearing up the sales force and succeeding in increasing the group sales budget. Training programmes for sales staff had also been set up, with incentives for good performers in the shape of silver and gold certificates.

There was a renewed effort to raise the level of sales achieved direct with customers, rather than through merchants, in an attempt to improve profitability further. At the same time the company began to offer an advisory service for architects and customers on both the design of brickwork and pre-cast applications.

There was also further in-house experimentation on methods of construction, including some of the industrialised techniques adopted on the continent. It was also decided to place a fresh emphasis on the production of hand-made bricks, for which demand was rising. At Aldridge a new plant prepared to start production of clay pavers for use in patios, precincts and on forecourts.

Increasingly Ibstock was coming to be seen as a recognisable producer of quality bricks, offering a brand product with a comprehensive range of alternatives and backed up by a national sales and distribution force.

"Brick began to travel increasingly long distances. Part of the appeal to architects was to be able to use something different, something not available in the locality. We were always on hand to provide technical advice and were ready to go on site to help solve any problems," recalls Tony King.

On a broader front Tony Cadman at the BDA had by now completed his detailed analysis of the state of the brick sector and began to tour the country impressing upon producers the scale of the industry's problems and trying to convince them of the need for urgent action.

By now he had talked to Government and to the architects, many of whom still tended to dismiss the product as a Victorian relic incapable of providing the opportunities offered by concrete. The Ministry of Housing was similarly unimpressed and remained committed to the extensive use of industrialised building methods in the building sector.

Cadman was convinced that the answer to such antagonism lay in appealing direct to the ultimate user of brick - the general public. His plan was to create an image for brick which those responsible for building would not be able to ignore.

Early in 1972 he had thought of a simple yet attractive slogan which encapsulated the approach which he and a few of the industry's leaders supported. It was "Brick is Beautiful" and it became one of the most potent marketing phrases of the day.

The intention was to portray brick as a superior building material, endlessly flexible in its application and environmentally beyond reproach. According to Cadman: "By pushing brick into the public consciousness we wanted to frighten the professions into action. I exposed myself to every possible media opportunity to get the message across."

Cadman and his bricks got millions of pounds worth of free air time to expound on a philosophy which Ibstock, if not every brickmaker, heartily endorsed.

MPs were recruited to the cause to help get the message across to Government while the brick producers began to dig deep into their pockets to finance a marketing drive. The direct result was an increase in selling prices to customers, which brought fears that bricks would merely price themselves out of an already highly-competitive market place.

The director general was well aware that his activities provoked a nervous reaction among some of his masters, though he singles out Paul Hyde-Thomson for his unruffled support and encouragement when the going got rough. "Paul's diplomacy kept some of the Association's members from calling a halt to the campaign. He spent a lot of time travelling around the country, pouring oil on troubled waters."

Jeremy Rowe of London Brick, who was to precede Hyde-Thomson as BDA chairman, looks back on the Cadman appointment as a "brave decision."

He recalls: "His favourite phrase was any publicity is good

publicity. It was all very stimulating stuff and certainly helped raise the profile of the brick industry as well as that of Tony Cadman himself. He got us back on the map."

Cadman himself never doubted that the campaign would succeed. Looking back he says it was clear after two years that his five-year plan had already succeeded in restoring brick's self-confidence and raising the industry's profile. "I had done my homework and knew we had a superior product. The challenge was to crack the facade of political idiocy and to overcome the folly surrounding structural and design fashions at the time. We had to point out to the public what they were having to endure and what alternatives were available."

As Cadman got into his stride Ibstock continued to benefit from the buoyant market which survived throughout 1972. As an added bonus the group's wood pulp agency division also began to emerge from a long period of depressed demand.

The end of the year saw Johnsen, Jorgensen and Wettre embark on a partnership venture with the formation of Crusader Board Merchants, a Woolwich-based business engaged in the merchanting and reprocessing of board used for packaging consumer goods.

The proposal had been put forward to Richard Johnsen by Desmond Martin and Bayliss Barnett, who had identified the potential for a comprehensive service of board conversion, stockholding and merchanting which they believed would be welcome to major board mills and to customers in the packaging industry. The business would eventually be sold off, however.

By Christmas 1972 Ibstock was brimming with confidence over its new-found strength and the commercial opportunities which lay ahead. The chairman was soon able to tell shareholders that the group envisaged boosting brick production from around 200 million to 375 million - at a cost of about £13m - over the next five years.

There was also a brief, but intriguing, reference to a study of business prospects for the group within the markets of the European Economic Community. Ibstock had not even started on the most ambitious phase of its history.

8

A toe in Europe

ALMOST unnoticed during the hectic spell of takeovers which had continued throughout 1972, the Ibstock board had called for a report on the brick market in West Germany.

By August Hyde-Thomson and Tony King had also visited a Dutch brick maker to see its brick panel production facilities and, just as importantly, to assess its potential as a possible candidate for a takeover.

As Britain prepared, finally, to enter the European Economic Community, Ibstock was ready to use its national standing as the launch-pad for its own expedition into Europe. According to Richard Boxall - who had joined the group in 1968 as general manager at Aldridge, moved to do the same job at Ibstock and was about to become group production director - the prospect caused considerable excitement.

In his view: "There was a determination, despite the recent spate of expansion, not to get too big in the domestic brick market. Ibstock wanted to stay at the premium end of the facing brick business. The view was that, the bigger we got, the more like the average producer we were bound to become."

The logical step was to seek business in other new markets, though not everyone in the group was happy about the prospect. Some directors still remembered with a shudder the chairman's plan to link up with a producer in Iran and to export Ibstock's production know-how and sales methods to carve out a share of a growing market. The deal had never materialised and the ensuing chaos in Iran had demonstrated the potential dangers of moving away from familiar and well-tested markets in search of new hunting grounds.

Europe was clearly different, however, and in early 1973 - as Ibstock Building Products replaced Ibstock Brick & Tile as the holding company for the building products division - the search was on. For a while hopes were high that a deal could be done with Delta Baksteen, a Dutch brick and brick panel maker that had been visited the previous autumn. The company produced 100 million bricks a year, one quarter of which were exported to other countries.

Delta at first declared an interest in a possible sale but subsequently, despite the efforts of the Ibstock chairman and Michael Keeling, set its face against takeover by a foreign company. Assisted by Michael Keeling and Richard Boxall, the chairman began flying to Holland - West Germany had been discounted because of language problems and accountancy differences - on reconnaissance trips.

By mid-summer the chairman was able to report that he had two companies in his sights, one of them by the name of Van Wijcks Waalsteenfabrieken, a high-quality facing brick manufacturer located close to Arnhem in the province of Gelderland.

The plant, standing between the winter dyke protecting the village of Heteren and the River Rhine, occupied a 45-acre site along with 122 acres of clay-bearing land and numerous other parcels of freehold land. Bricks had first been made at Heteren in the late 18th Century by the Van Geijn family, whose interests had later passed to the Van Wijck family.

The factory was destroyed during the Battle of Arnhem in the Second World War but it had risen from the ashes and, by the early 1970s, the company's 73 employees were engaged in producing around 50 million bricks a year. A major investment programme had included a new tunnel kiln, the commissioning of which, in early 1973, had hit output and left the company facing temporary losses.

In the longer term, however, the business was blessed with unusually large clay supplies which would guarantee production for another 30 years or more. Many Dutch producers had no more than two or three years' reserves and were forced to buy in their clay requirements.

In 1972 Van Wijcks had sold 27 million bricks to Holland, West Germany and Belgium, having been produced in the Ibstock manner from an extruded clay column rather than by the more usual Dutch "soft mud" process of machine moulding. The plant also employed a tunnel kiln as well as a chamber kiln, which had been made by Keller, the German supplier of the Aldridge unit.

Hyde-Thomson was a great deal more keen on the business than he was on the bumpy rides which he had endured by light aircraft across the English Channel in search of pastures new. A deal costing Ibstock £1.31m was struck and completed in October 1973 and all parties involved expressed high hopes that the pooling of British and Dutch resources would provide a winning blend.

Attention briefly switched to more domestic issues following an announcement by the Government that it had decided to investigate the supply of building bricks and to establish whether a monopoly situation existed.

The decision had been provoked by the increasing dominance of London Brick, already the subject of earlier inquiries by the National Board for Prices and Incomes. The group by now accounted for around 43 per cent of the total output of bricks but, more significantly, it also controlled about 95 per cent of all fletton production, a position it had steadily achieved through organic growth and via acquisitions.

By the time the Monopolies Commission stepped in, London Brick had only two surviving rivals, neither of which was destined to remain independent for much longer. Though the non-fletton producers appeared to have little to worry about, the prospect of an inquiry which was set to last for three years was the source of some concern.

On behalf of the industry the BDA at once issued a statement offering wholehearted co-operation to the Commission and singing the brickmakers' praises. It pointed out that, in the previous three years, brick production had risen sharply, from 6.5 billion in 1971 to an estimated 7.5 billion in 1973.

The BDA emphasised that over the previous decade the industry had invested heavily in modern plant, raising productivity and reducing the labour force. At the same time, it claimed, manufacturers had tried hard to increase the market for bricks in the non-housing sector, competing against materials such as concrete, glass, steel, plastic wood and aluminium.

In a carefully worded piece of special pleading, the statement concluded: "If the report of the Monopolies Commission once again spells out difficulties created by fluctuations in the level of house building for a capital intensive, mechanised and mass production industry such as brickmaking, then the report will be of value to the industry."

As the industry digested the implications of another investigation, Ibstock at once put the seal on its second European purchase and established Ibstock International to act as the vehicle for its burgeoning overseas businesses.

This time the spotlight was on Maatschappij tot Exploitatie van Steenfabrieken Udenhout, voorheen Weyers, Holland's only publicly-quoted brick maker with two factories in the south of the country, at Udenhout and at Maren. The company also owned rights to clay extraction on several hundred acres of land.

A 49.9 per cent stake in the company was held by Jessel Europa, the Dutch subsidiary of UK-based Jessel Securities, which had alienated the company by quietly acquiring its interest. Faced with threats of mass resignations from within the company, the unwelcome shareholder was willing to sell for just over £500,000.

Like Van Wijcks, the business offered an annual capacity of 50 million bricks, including a range of hand-made lines. It appeared to be well-run under the watchful eye of Dirk Wesseling, the English-speaking managing director whose previous high-ranking career in the civil service had given him responsibility for the Dutch construction sector.

Wesseling recalls Ibstock's arrival on the scene: "Brick had never been marketed in Holland and Ibstock wanted to repeat the formula which was proving increasingly successful in its own market. "Being the perfect gentleman, Paul Hyde-Thomson told my board that he was being offered the Jessel stake in the business. He wanted to know if we objected. If we did not, then he would expect a seat on the board."

There were no objections and the deal was done. Almost at once Ibstock picked up sufficient additional shares to give it a controlling interest in the business. The balance was purchased in May the following year.

The six stages of brick, from clay extraction through firing to final use.

Claywinning.

Delivery to the grinding and making plant.

Extruding a column of processed clay.

Fired bricks leaving the kiln.

Delivery to site.

Finished brickwork.

Together Ibstock's new acquisitions made it the sixth largest brick producer in the Netherlands, owning three factories with a combined annual capacity of 100 million bricks. Within 150 kilometres lived a market of 40 million potential customers.

There were those, like Jim Donaldson, who had their doubts about prospects for the company in Europe but who nevertheless pulled out all the stops to make the venture a success. Despatched to Van Wijcks to help bring Ibstock discipline to a shambles of a factory, he and Wesseling, who had almost at once been put in charge of both acquisitions, got down to work.

A new factory was planned but one of the first initiatives was the removal of the Van Wijcks stockpile of unsold bricks. According to Wesseling: "We had 14 million lousy bricks standing in the yard which were scaring customers away. We sold them off at cut-throat prices and made a fresh start. It took us a couple of years to convince customers that we were offering quality bricks again."

Donaldson himself was to retire at the start of 1974 but he would continue to advise the group on its Dutch operations for another two years. It was not until some time later that

Seedlings under glass

A Eucalyptus forest

Drying the pulp

Packaged ready for despatch

Ibstock's other arm. Pulp for paper making, from seedlings under glass to the packaged product ready for sale.

Ibstock's Dutch adventure was to turn sour.

If the Dutch businesses got off to an encouraging start, conditions in the domestic market were to take a dramatic turn for the worse during the winter of 1973 and the first few months of 1974. Ibstock, like every other participant in the nation's economy, found themselves at the mercy of events beyond their control.

In November, as the miners began an overtime ban in support of their claim for higher pay and better conditions, the Organisation of Petroleum Exporting Countries announced an initial doubling in the price of crude oil, heralding the beginning of an international energy crisis which was to have permanent repercussions on the world's economic communities.

As though that were not enough, the miners' action brought power shortages to Britain and, in December, Edward Heath's Government was forced to introduce a three-day working week for industry in an attempt to ration electricity supplies.

There were also cuts in public expenditure which, combined with high interest rates, put a sharp brake on housebuilding activity, the source of a little less than half of Ibstock's brick business. By February 1974 the miners had withdrawn their labour and Heath went down to a general election defeat on the question "Who rules Britain?"

Ibstock's chairman told shareholders that the national state of emergency had made new demands on the business but he praised his employees for their "magnificent" response to the situation. Through the dark days of the first three months of 1974 the group managed to maintain output at 70 per cent of normal levels. By the middle of the year, by which time the group had organised an increase in its borrowing powers, total profits were running 10 per cent below the level achieved a year earlier, a position which would have been worse but for successful trading on the wood pulp business, which by now was referred to as the fibres division.

In a reference to a political situation in which Harold Wilson governed without an overall majority in the House of Commons, the chairman stressed that confidence in the economy would only return when there was "real and respected leadership in the country."

On the continent Ibstock's new businesses had not got off to a particularly auspicious start in the face of deteriorating market conditions and mounting stocks. The cumulative result was a temporary halt in 1974 to the group's steadily rising profits record, with pre-tax profits slipping back to £2m.

Although Himley, Ibstock and Aldridge improved profits, there were problems at Roughdales, with the company forced to implement a rare round of redundancies affecting 38 men. Group brick sales from Ibstock's eight UK factories fell from a peak of 195 million in 1973 to 143 million. It reached 84 million in Europe.

The year had been one in which survival had been the name of the game and Ibstock had, at least, done better than most in holding its own. One casualty of the difficult conditions was new spending. The board decided to shelve the balance of its ambitious investment programme following the completion of the new factories at Nostell and Cattybrook.

The next 12 months were to see no end to the nation's economic problems, with the recession pushing unemployment up beyond the one million mark. It was, by Ibstock's recent standards, to be a quiet year, with no takeovers and all efforts concentrated on combatting the depressed levels of demand from customers.

It was just such market conditions which put Ibstock's trading philosophy to the test. In the middle of the year, in an attempt to streamline and reinforce its sales network, Graham Walker announced the creation of five regional sales offices based at the group's principal works.

Selling had never been more vital and the regional sales managers - Dilwyn Price in the north, Alan Butler in the East Midlands, Geoff Yates in the West Midlands, Andrew McEwan in the south west, Peter Bray in the north east and Vernon Hanlon in London - found themselves at the sharp end of Ibstock's efforts.

The company also decided that the time was ripe to launch a special promotion of its special-shaped bricks, with less emphasis given to the hand-made lines for which labour was increasingly hard to find. In a blaze of publicity, embracing everything from car stickers to seminars, Ibstock vigorously marketed a product which offered the company higher margins and the customer a new dimension to the use of brick.

Sometimes there was less success in generating the same sort of interest at the brickworks, where "specials" meant disruption to the normal production run. Eventually, in another pioneering move for the industry, their production would be left to specially-designed off-line kilns within the group's works.

Before long salesmen were also equipped with special-shape kits containing miniature examples of what the group could offer and demonstrating to architects the endless versatility and flexibility of the products. Many potential customers were to delight in building desk-top projects with the new sales toy.

Measures to improve quality control were also stepped up and all the group's employees - for the first time exceeding 1,000 - were involved in the drive to increase Ibstock's share of whatever market was available.

The strategy worked well. Towards the end of 1975 housing activity picked up, helping national deliveries of facing bricks to end the year up by more than 10 per cent, although they remained one-fifth lower than at the start of the decade. Ibstock's own deliveries, however, increased by more than 35 per cent. While the profits of some competitors fell or remained flat, Ibstock managed to push theirs up to £2.58m.

At the year-end the board was sufficiently confident to reactivate its planned investment programme. In mid-November the directors told shareholders there were plans to spend several million pounds, principally in the UK, to maintain group modernisation and development.

The announcement was by way of an explanation for a rights issue through Laing & Cruickshank, intended to raise funds for the next stages of Ibstock's expansion. Shareholders were offered a one-for-three share issue, raising £1.4m. Two weeks before Christmas the money was in the bank.

Hyde-Thomson told shareholders: "Ibstock is taking the lead in planning this growth, whilst much of British industry continues to be criticised for its lack of investment. One of the reasons cited for the run-down of many of our key industries is this continued under-investment, which results in outdated manufacturing plant, leading eventually to its non-profitability, which in turn leads to loss of jobs."

Having spent over £7m in three years in equipping itself for the future, Ibstock was hardly in line for criticism on that count.

The year 1976 dawned no brighter for the national economy. By the autumn the Government would face a sterling crisis as overseas confidence in Britain plunged. Labour Chancellor Denis Healey was obliged to implement a four per cent pay ceiling and to call in the International Monetary Fund to help salvage Britain's finances and its reputation.

Ibstock defiantly cast its sights ahead to the better days and higher demand it eventually expected. As the Monopolies Commission report was published, concluding that London Brick's monopoly was not operating against the public interest, Ibstock was demonstrably expressing its confidence in the future. The group, said the chairman, intended to go on increasing its share of the market and had decided to bring back into use plant which had been lying idle.

The aim was to raise output by around 20 million bricks to 210 million - an objective which was to be achieved. Profits also rose substantially to reach £3.72m on deliveries of 206 million bricks. Despite the continuing doldrums in the housing sector Ibstock was continuing to pick up major contracts from important industrial clients.

In another challenging year the group managed to provide bricks for a range of projects which embraced construction of the Berkeley nuclear power station near Bristol, BBC Television studios near Cardiff and a uranium enrichment plant in Cheshire. On the pre-cast side, which was yet to hit hard times, contracts included the Unilever library and conference centre in Bedfordshire and the National Westminster Bank computer centre in the City.

In Holland, too, demand improved, although with severe price controls in existence the opportunity for improving profits was limited. Brick production from the group's three Dutch factories topped 100 million, with sales reaching 108 million.

Dirk Wesseling had, by now, assimilated Ibstock's marketing methods and increasing attention was being paid to industrial, rather than residential, builders. "We started going direct to the customers, who were beginning to believe that our bricks were worth having again." Export business to West Germany was also going well.

At the very end of 1976, as the British Cabinet agreed to a package of expenditure cuts in order to obtain further credit from the IMF, Ibstock again donned its takeover hat and acquired the assets of Hudson Brick and Engineering, a subsidiary of Grendon Trust, which had shortly before been close to liquidation.

The business had two plants in Sussex, at West Hoathly and Laybrook, with a combined, annual capacity of 25 million bricks. For £1.3m Ibstock also acquired a small engineering works at West Hoathly and a dormant brick works at Horam. A business which had made pre-tax profits of £260,000 in the previous year also owned 180 acres of land.

West Hoathly, the largest works, had been founded in 1880 by a Mr. Trayton Stevens and is believed to have been started to help provide bricks for the Bluebell Railway Line. In 1910, the works was acquired by Hudsons, a business then largely involved in household removal and storage. Laybrook had been acquired only in 1961.

The deal filled another important gap in Ibstock's UK marketing plan, adding a further dimension to its product range and providing representation in another important regional market.

Early in the New Year the group prepared for its next acquisition. This time the deal was on the other side of the English Channel and it was to take Ibstock into another new market.

With an eye on increased production capacity and broader European markets, Ibstock went to Belgium and found Tuileries et Briqueteries d'Hennuyeres et de Wanlin, which had been founded in 1919 and which, until 1970, had remained under family management. It was quoted on the Belgian stock exchange but, at the end of January 1977, had ceased trading because of heavy losses.

The business operated two factories, the principal works located at Hennuyeres, 30 kilometres south of Brussels and close to the site of the Battle of Waterloo, where it held extensive clay reserves and operated a modern tunnel kiln as well as an old chamber kiln. It had been the expense incurred in installing the new kiln, together with an automatic tile press, which had brought the company to its knees, leaving it with large stocks and serious liquidity problems.

The plant manufactured a range of clay products, mainly roofing tiles, hollow blocks and bricks. The second factory was situated at Wanlin to the south east of the Belgian capital, where two old chamber kilns produced around eight million high-quality facing bricks a year. Though Ibstock could not have known it, this small plant would, within a few years, represent the group's only remaining foothold in continental Europe.

At the time of their purchase the two Belgian plants provided an annual capacity of 40 million bricks which Ibstock promptly purchased for just under £1m. Once production was restarted the new owners began to convert spare capacity at the main works to produce quality facing bricks, upon which the emphasis was firmly placed. The bricks manufactured would be used to complement the output of the Dutch factories.

Within weeks the group had spent more funds, this time on the purchase of Steenfabriek De Ruiterwaard, which operated three factories 30 kilometres to the south of Utrecht, at Gameren, Tricht and Herwijnen. Once again the intention was to provide extra production capacity and to widen the group's customer base.

The Gameren site had a tunnel kiln with an annual production capacity of 150,000 sq. metres of floor tiles while the Tricht factory's tunnel kiln was capable of producing nearly 25 million bricks a year as well as 32,000 sq. metres of tiling. At Herwijnen, the plant could produce nearly 19 million hand-made bricks a year.

The deal arose partially out of Dirk Wesseling's need to recruit someone who could mastermind the marketing drive in Europe. That man, in his eyes, was Maarten Janssens, a somewhat extrovert manager who ran De Ruiterwaarde and its workforce of 40 on behalf of family interests. In the first year Ibstock more than recovered the modest purchase price in profits.

Now the English brick specialist had six factories in Holland which would both produce and sell 154 million bricks in their first year under the same corporate roof. A growing number of Ibstock bricks were also being exported from the UK to meet orders taken by the Dutch subsidiaries.

There were some early prestige contracts. In the first year under new management the Dutch businesses won orders to supply bricks for the renovation of the former palace of Queen Wilhelmina at Apeldoorn and for the construction of a stadium for PSV Eindhoven, one of Holland's most successful football clubs. There was also a one million brick consignment to the Belgian army.

Between them the Dutch plants - soon to be brought beneath the Ruga Beheer marketing umbrella - held around seven per cent of the total Dutch market for bricks. According to Wesseling: "We aimed everything at the top end of the market, where our share was much bigger. It turned out to be dangerously big."

Ibstock was by now on the trail of orders even further afield. In the Middle East, for example, building activity remained intense and, largely due to the efforts of Andrew Presho, the export manager, Ibstock bricks were being sold into the United Arab Emirates and used by Indian and Egyptian bricklayers in a range of commercial and housing contracts.

Group pre-tax profits for 1977 rose again to more than £4m, despite tough times for a fibres division battling against a recession in world pulp markets. Even so it managed to record sales of £27m during the year, a suitably impressive note on which to mark the departure of Roy Johnsen as chairman and managing director of Johnsen, Jorgensen and Wettre after 41 years with the company. Brother Peter assumed the role.

Just before Christmas, as Dirk Wesseling and Richard Boxall, now managing director of Ibstock Building Products, prepared to take their places on the Ibstock Johnsen board, time caught up with Ibstock Precast. Boxall revealed that losses had been building up for some time and with the outlook for orders remaining poor, the directors had decided to terminate what, at one stage, had appeared to be a highly promising commercial initiative. Forty five redundancies followed.

But if Ibstock found itself uncharacteristically divesting itself of a small number of personnel, the group's 2,000-strong payroll was about to swell by one-third in a move which was spectacularly ambitious and which would put to the test every ounce of skill and experience it possessed.

9

A Foothold in North America

TOWARDS the end of 1977 Paul Hyde-Thomson had travelled to the United States to attend a convention of the Brick Institute of America. It would prove to be the start of something big.

The conference provided US producers with an annual opportunity to meet and discuss the latest trends and developments in their industry and overseas visitors were always welcome to participate, to learn and compare their own experiences with those of their American colleagues.

Hyde-Thomson, however, had a more specific mission in mind. With the group's European acquisitions safely under its belt and beginning to perform well, he calculated that it was capable of taking the next logical step - that of extending its international operations to a market which consumed eight billion bricks every year.

True, the challenge of running a business on the other side of the Atlantic would be a giant leap compared with its cross-channel exploits but the principal was the same. There was a huge market to be fulfilled and Ibstock's style of business might offer a formula for further success.

To the chairman, whose reserved demeanour belied his

ambition to expand the Ibstock business still further, the idea of a US business appeared increasingly attractive. Having tried to get a foothold in Canada, he now directed his attention further to the south.

He came away from the BIA convention convinced that Ibstock could and should enter the US market. His inquiries had shown that the US brick industry had a lacklustre record of profitability, that marketing was left to the distributors and that the price of brick, which was highly thought of as a building material, was often relatively low.

Ibstock was not keen, however, on beginning with another Hennuyeres-type recovery situation. It wanted a business which was large enough and sufficiently established to provide a firm base from which to trade up and which would benefit from its marketing skills and profit-oriented approach.

Hyde-Thomson had a clear picture in his mind about the sort of candidate which would fit the bill. It would operate modern plant, be grouped reasonably close together and would preferably have an annual capacity of more than 225 million bricks. The price tag would have to be in the region of £5m.

The chairman had done enough homework to know that few US brickmakers fitted the bill. There was Acme Brick, the largest US manufacturer, which was based in Texas and produced 850 million bricks annually, more than twice that of Ibstock in the UK and on the continent. The other companies on Ibstock's potential "hit list" were General Shale of Tennessee, Glen-Gery Corporation of Pennsylvania, which Richard Boxall had already visited in order to see its coal-fired operations, Boren Clay Products of North Carolina, Belden Brick of Ohio and Bickerstaff Clay Products, based in Georgia.

There was a also a subsidiary list of manufacturers which Ibstock had identified as being of possible interest. They included companies in Texas, Virginia and Iowa and one by the name of Marion Brick of Ohio, a subsidiary since 1972 of the Cleveland-based Medusa Portland Cement.

The chairman's favourite, however, was General Shale, a publicly-quoted corporation with 10 plants providing a capacity of 525 million bricks annually. Sales of around £19m a year were producing profits of a little over £3m.

One of Shale's biggest assets was George Sells, its president and chief executive, and something of a "guru" in the US brick industry. By the start of 1978 Hyde-Thomson had told his Ibstock board colleagues that General Shale would be an ideal company to "trade up," providing it could win control.

In April 1978 Sells found himself on a visit to Britain and having dinner at Stable House, the chairman's home at North Kilworth in Leicestershire. Tony King and Richard Boxall were also invited. Sells' hosts were anxious to hear what he thought of their plans to move into the US and whether he could nominate any businesses which might fit the bill.

It was not General Shale itself, however, which dominated the conversation but Marion Brick, the Ohio-based operation which, he said, was on the market and had already been the subject of one bid.

Marion had been established in 1950 as Keramos - the Greek word for ceramics - with one plant at Morral, Ohio, a small farming community at the heart of the state. It had grown steadily since its formation, adding new plant, with the latest purchased in 1975.

As Scott Rogers, the President of Medusa, arrived in his office on April 10, he received a telephone call from England. Hyde-Thomson was direct, asking if the Marion business was for sale and how much the owners were likely to want for it. Rogers confirmed that Medusa had already rejected a $7m offer from Canada Brick and said that, while Medusa had big plans for its cement business, it was anxious to divest itself of a brickmaking operation which it did not understand and which, with pre-tax profits running at nearly $2m a year, was too small to retain. If Ibstock was interested, Medusa would be happy to talk.

The chairman did not wait for a second invitation, flying Concorde to New York where he met bankers to establish that credit would be available if any sale was agreed. He flew on to Cleveland and to a 7am breakfast meeting with Medusa directors. In the next two days Hyde-Thomson visited all the plants as well as the head office at Marion, accompanied by Rogers as well as Herb Anderson, Marion's President and other executives.

Before returning home he tried unsuccessfully to extract from the Americans an idea of the sort of price which would bring Marion into the Ibstock fold. Undaunted the chairman reported to the board that Marion was up for grabs and that the opportunity to establish a US foothold would not last for long. He recommended a bid of up to $10m and, with his colleagues' agreement, called for a quick financial investigation of the Cleveland business.

A separate market research exercise was also commissioned from Robert Hayes and Associates, which by May had confirmed what Ibstock wanted to hear.

It concluded that the US brick market held enormous potential, with evidence suggesting that an increasing number of customers would prefer to buy direct from the manufacturers rather than relying on the dealers who did not believe they had any significant role to play in influencing the decision-making process involved in the choice of construction materials.

Tony King, who would soon be chairman of Ibstock's first American business, told his colleagues: "Conditions in the US market appear likely to be receptive to an aggressive and imaginative marketing programme."

Negotiations began with Marion and, by the first week in June, agreement had been reached. The final cash price was $9m (£4.9m) and Ibstock's first beachhead in the US was secured. "Now We're In The USA!" ran the headline in Ibstock News, the group newspaper.

For its money the British company had acquired seven facing brick plants in four north-eastern states. The choice of region was no accident given the group's conclusion that, although the construction sector in the area appeared to be more architecturally sophisticated, brick producers had failed to make an impact on the specifiers of building materials. As a result they had been rapidly dying off.

Within Marion there were two plants at Brazil, Indiana, producing up to 76 million bricks a year and, apart from the original Morral unit, there was another Ohio plant at Caledonia, together adding an additional capacity of 67 million bricks. Two more factories with a combined annual output of up to 57 million bricks were located at Clearfield and Bigler in Pennsylvania.

The tally was completed with a single plant at Manassas in Virginia, where Marion produced a further 50 million bricks. Though some of the units had their own supplies of raw material, others bought in from local suppliers. A fairly wide range of buff and red extruded products was available, though exclusively through dealers and distributors.

Together Marion handed Ibstock an annual capacity of 250 million facing bricks, virtually the same volume it had produced within the UK during the previous year. The deal promised to increase group turnover by about one quarter and total production by more than a half.

There were also another 590 employees on a group payroll which now numbered nearly 2,500, nearly half of which was overseas. It was a giant leap which marked a major milestone in the development of the group. But if there were any private reservations within the board about the advisability of such an ambitious initiative, coming so soon after the move into continental Europe, they did not surface.

Shareholders were told that Marion's management would be retained and that, in an attempt to reduce dependence on a volatile housing sector - which took 70 per cent of sales - the emphasis would switch to marketing its products as quality architectural materials with countless applications.

The timing appeared perfect. As control changed hands the US housing market was in the middle of a construction boom. More than two million homes had been started in 1977 and the total was about to be repeated in 1978. Armour Johnson, head of Marion's sales operation, summed up the market situation by telling employees that the company faced a major problem in producing sufficient bricks to keep brick-hungry dealers happy.

In the first month under Ibstock, Marion managed to despatch no fewer than 24 million bricks, reducing stocks by five million and making an early contribution to trading profits.

By September the scale of the transformation of Ibstock's business was made clear in remarks by the chairman, who said it appeared probable that combined turnover for Europe and the US during 1978 would exceed that in the UK. By the end of the year the group had produced a total of nearly 400 million bricks in its European and American factories, compared with 250 million in the UK.

Profits for the year topped £5m for the first time and, yet again, Ibstock had managed to buck the normal brick cycle, with its formula of running production flat out, keeping pressure on unit costs and picking up market share from more hesitant competitors.

The beginning of 1979 brought a harsh winter on both sides of the Atlantic, with the overseas businesses only managing to despatch roughly two-thirds of production, compared with 100 per cent a year earlier. In the first half stocks rose by over 85 million, depriving the group of around £1m in profits.

Margins suffered, courtesy of Marion , while the Belgian operation was heading for losses of over £1m for the year as the new owners struggled to improve management, streamline production and to push up sales. But although the financial press spoke of an understandable period of consolidation ahead, Ibstock was about to confound the analysts with another, even more audacious, takeover.

This time it wanted Glen-Gery Corporation, the Pennsylvania-based facing brick manufacturer which had figured in the chairman's original "hit list" of potential acquisition.

Glen-Gery was, by American standards, a long-established business. It had been founded as the Montello Brick Company in 1890 by one A.A Gery, who had previously tried his hand at newspapers and real estate.

His business had developed steadily to the point where it operated six brick manufacturing plants, two concrete block making factories and an anthracite processing company. Brick, however, had always been its primary business, the plants producing wire-cut products and moulded brick, of which it claimed to be the largest US manufacturer. Some units also produced brick paving and an attractive line of hand-made bricks.

The business was based half way between Washington and New York, at Reading, Pennsylvania, the State within which all its manufacturing centres were based. Located at Wyomissing, Shoemakersville, Watsontown, York and New Oxford, which had two units, the plants had a combined annual capacity of 270 million bricks. In the previous year, Glen-Gery had made pre-tax profits of just under £2m on turnover of £15m.

In charge of the business was Douglas Mault, the president, who had been brought in by Canadian businessman Saul Simkin, the majority shareholder in Glen-Gery. His appointment had followed a traumatic parting of the ways with the previous chief executive, whose dictatorial ways had left what one Ibstock director would later describe as "a terrible culture" within the company.

Ibstock proceeded to negotiate smoothly the purchase of Simkin's 58 per cent stake in the business and, on July 4 - as brick sales in the US began to slip - it announced an offer for the balance of the equity which valued the entire business at $21m (£9.6m).

Simultaneously shareholders were informed that they would shortly be asked to provide help towards meeting the cost of the purchase via a rights issue intended to raise nearly £5m and to take some of the pressure off a balance sheet carrying sharply increased borrowings.

Now Ibstock owned a US brickmaking capacity of more than 500 million a year, spread between 13 plants in one of the most concentrated and prosperous markets of the country. The twin deals had handed the group five per cent of the entire US facing brick market and made it the largest producer of quality facing bricks in a region with 100 million potential customers. It was heady, if challenging, stuff and the task of producing a united team with a positive marketing policy began at once.

But Ibstock's new strength was greeted with somewhat less enthusiasm in some other circles; the deal did not please everyone, as later events would eventually demonstrate.

There were other problems on the horizon. In October, just as the group was disappointing the stock market with a forecast of a 10 per cent drop in profits for 1979, it launched its two-for-five rights issue to shareholders. A total of 7.9m new shares were put on offer through Laing and Cruickshank at 65p per share - the day before the announcement they stood at 82p - and were underwritten by London and Yorkshire Trust.

In the eyes of the City the timing was highly unfortunate. The view from the Square Mile was that the group had been over-optimistic in assessing the financing costs of its second US deal and that the continuing losses in Belgium, where it believed "radical surgery" was overdue, were increasingly unacceptable.

But Ibstock still had a great many friends and admirers. The financial press, while acknowledging that the short-term prospects for the group looked uncharacteristically muted, appeared confident that a rally was around the corner in 1980.

Even so when details of the rights issue take-up were revealed in mid-November, there was no escaping the fact that the exercise had proved an embarrassing flop. With the group's shares having fallen in the intervening weeks below the rights issue price, shareholders took up only 44 per cent of the stock on offer.

Ibstock described the issue's failure as a casualty of market conditions at the time. London & Yorkshire had to step in and buy what no-one else apparently wanted.

By the year-end, however, the US business was beginning to reflect the Ibstock philosophy. Already, it was being shaped along the lines of the group's other operations, offering customers as comprehensive a range of brick types as possible, continuity of quality and a strategy which placed as much emphasis on support services as it did on the products themselves.

In one interview the chairman summed up the challenge to which Ibstock had already responded on the other side of the Atlantic: "One of our main objectives is to make people appreciate how exciting brick can be. We are essentially trying to help architects express their dreams in brick and there can be few places with more potential for doing that than the United States."

The group wasted little time in capitalising on the scope for raising the prices of such an invaluable aid to imaginative and attractive construction. Its market research had left it in no doubt that, although the gap between the price achieved by the brick maker and that charged to the end user was substantial, the advantage of such large margins was going not to the producer but to the army of middle-men distributors.

Hyde-Thomson added: "Our basic strategy has hinged on the assumption that if we can promote our product so that everyone begins to believe there really is no acceptable alternative, then we can get the price right."

The process of getting the price right was well underway by the end of 1979. At the time of the Marion takeover prices had averaged around $85 per thousand bricks but by now they were selling at around $100. More importantly, the margin between production costs and selling prices had widened from about $5 for every 1,000 bricks to as much as $15.

Not all Marion production was being sold but prices, in line with Ibstock policy, were being maintained. While the Marion operation had remained largely dependent on dealers, Glen-Gery was already beginning to sell direct to the specifiers.

There were other changes, too. A new chief executive had been appointed at Marion earlier in the year but Reynold Nebel, who was recruited from the asbestos industry, was not to stay long, following the acquisition of Glen-Gery and, with it, Doug Mault. According to Richard Boxall, then about to be appointed group operations director with particular responsibility for the US in place of a departing Tony King, the idea of the two men trying to run sister businesses alongside each other was "a recipe for disaster."

Nebel was paid off and, at the start of 1980, Mault was appointed president and chief executive of the combined US businesses to be run under the Glen-Gery Corporation banner.

In the event 1979 had not turned out quite as badly as the board had predicted at the time of the rights issue. In a year which saw the group purchase Lutterworth House - a listed, early 19th Century home which was to become its headquarters - and what the chairman described as a "mixed-bag of events and performances," pre-tax profits ended eight per cent lower at £4.68m.

Profits had been good in the UK, where Margaret Thatcher had become the first woman prime minister, promising to end the industrial decline and division which had become known as the "British disease."

In Holland, where the market was slackening, profits were down and in Belgium they were non-existent. In the United States, where Ibstock was now adding projects like the Gerald Ford Library in Michigan and a courthouse restoration scheme in Gettysburg, Pennsylvania, to its order books, there was a modest trading profit, most of which came from Glen-Gery.

But the buoyant picture for construction in the US was changing and deliveries were down by 15 per cent from the levels achieved by the two separate operations in the previous year.

Glen-Gery's headquarters in Reading, Pennsylvania, suitably clad in its own brick.

The reduction appeared to be greater than was justified by the overall decline in US construction activity. For the first time there were doubts among some Ibstock personnel that the group might just be starting to price itself out of a market which looked increasingly shaky. Perhaps it did not understand America as well as it had imagined.

In more than one respect Ibstock's confident vision of a bigger brighter future was about to turn into something more akin to a corporate nightmare.

Skyscraper brick. Worldwide Plaza, a 770-ft high building in New York City. This complex, which took three years to build, used more than 4m Glen-Gery bricks including many special shapes. It received the City's Annual Excellence in Masonry Award in 1989.

Skilful brick. Ibstock brick sculpture on the American Bank Computer Centre in Reading, Pennsylvania.

10

"Avoid Ibstock"

ALTHOUGH business at the beginning of 1980 got off to an encouraging start in Britain, Ibstock was faced with the irony of being let down by the overseas operations it had been so keen to acquire. On the Continent Ibstock's managerial and sales skills were being put through the hoop.

The continuing problems in Belgium meant that the inevitable could no longer be avoided and, reluctantly, the decision was taken to stem the debilitating flow of losses. Ibstock had never liked closing plant, and to be forced to shut down on mainland Europe, which it had stormed so recently with so much self-assurance, was doubly difficult.

Still plagued by production problems against the background of a tough market, the main brick plant at Hennuyeres was closed down and talks proceeded with a view to disposing of the brick and tile facilities to a Belgian consortium of public and private interests. A sale was to be agreed at the end of the year, with Ibstock retaining only its small, high-quality facing brick plant at Wanlin in the Ardennes.

It was the end of a chapter which, perhaps, should never have been opened. The Belgian business had required a level of investment which Ibstock could not contemplate and it had taken on a challenge the scale of which it had never really appreciated. According to Hyde-Thomson: "It was beyond us. We never came to terms with managing it properly. The whole exercise was a terrible mistake." In Holland the economy in the early months of 1980 was in increasingly dire straits, with escalating interest rates leading to what the chairman would later describe as "cut-throat" conditions.

Dirk Wesseling found himself at the centre, not of a spirited assault on a foreign market place but of an increasingly worrying damage-limitation exercise. "Demand was collapsing, largely because interest rates were hitting the housing sector. We found ourselves in the wrong market, selling bricks at prices considerably higher than those of our competitors. Contractors were fighting for orders, cutting prices and squeezing suppliers. The Ibstock Johnsen philosophy meant we had higher overheads in terms of salesmen and showroom space, and we were getting hurt more than most of the others."

As the position deteriorated, so the case for harsh, remedial action grew stronger. Before long some reduction in a workforce of around 500 seemed inevitable, despite the immense problems which Dutch law placed in the way of employers wishing to embark upon redundancies.

Wesseling believed that around 100 people would have to go and, deploying his civil service experience and his Government contacts to the full, began the protracted task of seeking a cut in the work force. Eventually the required reduction in manpower would be achieved, though it took a year to complete and proved highly expensive, with shopfloor workers upwards receiving a minimum one year's salary.

Traditionally when there had been a production surplus in Holland, it had been solved by the industry in a demonstration of co-operation the likes of which would have seemed impossible in Britain. The brick manufacturers would each contribute into a fund which would be used to subsidise those companies which were willing to cease production in order to reduce industry stocks.

Wesseling had himself been involved in earlier such agreements and decided the time had come to seek another. There was to be no repeat, however: "This time the brick industry's surplus was running at 30 per cent. The problem was simply too big to be tackled as it had been in the past."

As efforts to improve the position of the Dutch business

continued, there was more gloom in the US. Recession had set in and, by the summer, housing starts were plummeting from their two million peak to an annual rate of around 1.25 million. It was, by any standards, "one hell of a fall," according to Boxall.

By the end of June the American business had built up six-month losses of nearly £300,000, a figure which was swelled further by the addition of associated interest charges.

Three weeks later there was still more bad news in the shape of a totally unexpected and ominous announcement from Washington.

In a short but nevertheless explosive statement, the US Department of Justice announced that it had filed a civil anti-trust suit challenging Ibstock's takeover of Glen-Gery. The complaint claimed that the acquisition violated the Clayton Act, which prohibited anti-competitive mergers, and it went on to demand that the British group divested itself of its new US business.

The suit also alleged that the acquisition of Glen-Gery had eliminated competition in the sale of facing bricks between it and Marion and that the deal would increase concentration in the manufacturing and sale of bricks in the north-east region of the country.

Mr. Sandford Litvack, the assistant Attorney General in charge of the anti-trust division of the Department of Justice, said that, through its control of the two corporations, Ibstock Johnsen had become the largest manufacturer of facing bricks in the 13 north-eastern states and controlled about 20 per cent of the market. In addition the group was now claimed to be among the three largest facing brick producers in the entire US.

Ibstock Johnsen was well aware that anti-trust suits were a hazard of commercial life in the US, just as the potential always existed for a Monopolies Commission investigation in Britain, but it had not expected to find itself on the receiving end of one. It had been provoked by an aggrieved dealer who had decided to seek damages because the acquisition of Glen-Gery, with its new emphasis on selling direct, was threatening to deprive him of some of his traditional business.

Though the case would have to be proved, Ibstock made clear from the outset that it would fight every step of the way to avoid the unthinkable. The chairman was to the point: "If the Department of Justice persists with the anti-trust suit, we will oppose it vigorously," he said, adding: "We believe it has no basis whatsoever as we do not consider we are in breach of the official guidelines."

Later he told shareholders: "We believe that such mergers, far from being harmful, are beneficial in that they improve the choice and service for the customer and strengthen the industry's ability to compete with alternative cladding materials." Without such marriages, he added, the industry was likely to continue to decline, despite evidence of a strong consumer preference for brick.

It was a powerful case, warning of the possible collapse of the brick manufacturing sector in the face of powerful corporations producing competitive cladding alternatives.

Hyde-Thomson at once sought, and received, the help of the British Embassy in Washington, which he still remembers warmly for its speedy and valuable assistance. He was on holiday in Italy when the embassy reached him and suggested the time was right to state his case to the US Attorney General's office.

The chairman left at once for Washington. "Their help on timing and on the political background to the situation proved enormously helpful. It made a critical difference," he said later. His views made clear, Ibstock settled down for a long and tense wait.

As the group's overseas operations encountered growing difficulties, so the UK market began to deteriorate towards the end of 1980. Even so, its appetite for domestic expansion had been whetted and in August Ibstock acquired Sevenoaks Brickworks, which had figured on its regional shopping list for some time.

The business operated a small factory on the edge of Sevenoaks, about 30 miles from London. It had an annual capacity of five million bricks, which would augment the range of stock bricks from the group's factories in Sussex. David Jones, the chairman, joined the board of Ibstock Building Products in a non-executive capacity and the group now had 11 brickmaking plants in the UK.

In the search for cost savings the Aldridge plant was by now being converted, without being shut down, to fire on coal in place of liquified petroleum. Together, gas and oil had been the principal fuel sources for the industry for the previous 20 years.

While the brick industry consumed only 200,000 tonnes of coal annually, most of it going to London Brick, it was using the gas equivalent of up to 500,000 tonnes of coal, and 300,000 tons of oil. For years producers had claimed the two fuels had enabled them to cut labour costs and limit pollution to levels not possible with coal.

Now, all the old assumptions were about to be challenged by Ibstock following a detailed appraisal which had included a study of coal-firing plant in the US. It was a pioneering move for the brick industry. No-one, including Ibstock, could be sure just how efficient coal would prove for kiln firing and there was concern about how much the residual coal ash left on bricks would affect their finish.

The new coal-firing system cost nearly £500,000 - a £30,000 Government grant was made available because of its energy-saving qualities - and independent Government experts monitoring the scheme believed it would pay for itself in a little over two years. In fact, within a year of the conversion, energy efficiency would be improved by between 10 and 15 per cent.

Gordon Taylor, the general manager at Aldridge, was delighted with the results: "We proved conclusively that resistance to using coal as a primary fuel was misguided. We increased our energy efficiency and lowered our fuel bill in one fell swoop."

As the UK market became more difficult so Ibstock stepped up its marketing effort. The Crawford Street showroom in London was transformed into the first brickwork design centre to provide technical and specialist advice aimed at achieving the highest quality brickwork and, thereby, further enhancing its popularity. A similar centre was also opened in Manchester, the response to which endorsed Ibstock's search for excellence.

There was nothing particularly outstanding, however, about the group's overall performance in 1980. When the figures emerged, Ibstock Johnsen had an unusually disappointing story to tell. The headlines said it all - "Ibstock tumbles to £2.2m", "Long Haul Ahead for Ibstock."

There were few bright spots to report at the end of a year of worsening trade conditions in all the group's brick markets. Once again a slightly increased contribution to profits from the fibres division managed to offer some relief from an increasingly depressing picture.

The performance was, above all, still being weighed down by the high cost of interest charges - 50 per cent up on the previous year - associated mainly with the borrowings arising from the faltering US acquisitions.

In Britain trading profits changed little from the previous year, with sales dipping and stocks rising. In the US sales for Glen-Gery had reached only 60 per cent of capacity; as a result stocks at the year-end had soared by 99 million bricks, or around 40 per cent of annual output. There were modest profits.

With the anti-trust suit still hanging over the US operation Hyde-Thomson put a brave face on the outlook: "If brick is to do well in difficult times, it must be supported by established and sophisticated promotional and service-oriented procedures. In the greater part of our sales areas, these procedures are still in their infancy and need time to mature, but we are confident that, by the time conditions start to improve, we will be well placed to take advantage of the upturn."

In Holland, where the struggle for sales and profitability in a crumbling market was being repeated, the revelation of losses was accompanied by the hope that the worst would soon be over. Such hopes were to prove in vain.

By the start of 1981 Ibstock's plight was giving rise to speculation about the group's future. Even before the full extent of its poor performance in the previous year was known, there were suggestions that the problem might be resolved by takeover.

The group, undeniably, still showed great longer-term potential but it was immediately vulnerable and potentially open to attack at a time of weakness. The Investors' Chronicle intoned: "A bidder, though, would need to be brave, for the extent of the US problems is hard to measure and the anti-trust move is a real complication."

First-quarter production in the US reached a mere one-third of capacity. With the US business engaged in what appeared to be an increasingly unequal struggle and the need for tough action becoming daily more apparent, Glen-Gery parted company in May 1981 with Doug Mault. Unable to accept readily direction from his new British bosses, his short-lived association with Ibstock had proved difficult and unsuccessful.

He was replaced not by an American but by John Kerr, a UK accountant, who had already been transferred from London to help Mault. Previously he had been finance director of Ibstock Building Products before being made responsible for corporate finance and development within the group as a whole.

The time had arrived for unpleasant decisions and to admit to a few mistakes. Faced with a collapsing American market the British had resorted to a tried and tested formula which had served them well in their own country but which appeared increasingly ill-judged in the US.

At home Ibstock had become accustomed to compensating for cost increases with higher prices for customers. It had also been used to maintaining production in the face of falling demand, taking brick into stock and waiting patiently for the next uplift in demand.

The US brick manufacturers behaved differently, however. When times got tough they instinctively slashed prices and, as stocks rose, shut down capacity. It was a reaction which the newest players in the market should have observed and followed. Instead, they had adopted a British solution to an American problem and it had not worked.

It fell to Kerr, reporting directly back to Richard Boxall, to insist that the patient begin to take its medicine. In a message to Glen-Gery employees Kerr said one of his principal aims was to provide an element of stability to a business which had undergone numerous changes.

He stressed that the industry was having to cope with some of the most difficult trading conditions it had faced for many years. The company had record stocks which had to be cut in a carefully planned and well-managed way. He explained: "First, we need to turn brick into cash; it is as simple as that. Second, we want to have space in our yards for some of the new products which we need to produce for our customers."

According to Boxall, Kerr's contribution during 1981, as US housing starts fell further to just over one million, was invaluable: "He ran a very tight ship, cutting costs, shutting down a lot of excess capacity and reducing stock." Kerr cannot have been the most popular man around Glen-Gery's new headquarters building in downtown Reading but, by then, there were no alternatives open to him.

There was to be some good news from the US during the summer. It was three o'clock on a July morning when Hyde-Thomson's telephone rang at his bedside. His US lawyer apologised for the hour but excitedly announced that the Department of Justice had dropped, without notice or explanation, the anti-trust suit which had overshadowed Glen-Gery operations for almost exactly a year. The decision was to have a continuing influence on the US Government's subsequent attitude to takeovers in the brick sector.

Ibstock was also badly in need of an uplift in Holland,

where the outlook seemed grave. Graham Walker, now managing director of Ibstock Building Products and busy trying to produce maximum profitability out of continuing recession, was also spending some of his time taking a closer look at the problems on the other side of the Channel.

Outside consultants were appointed to strengthen the arm of the local management but the industry was facing an almost unparalleled crisis in which one-fifth of Holland's one hundred brick manufacturing plants would close in little more than a year. Housing starts fell by 60 per cent from the level recorded a year earlier and worse was on the way.

There were, at least, some hopes that the misfortunes of others might help Ruga Beheer's own chances of survival. Ibstock's chairman, for one, expressed the belief that the "competitive bloodbath" might be at its goriest and that conditions would soon improve.

By the end of 1981 those hopes looked increasingly slim given another sharp fall in sales and further intense pressure on selling prices. To add to the problems the Wanlin brick plant in Belgium was hit by a severe fire in November. Always profitable, however, a decision was taken to rebuild the factory and press on, using the local clay to manufacture in Holland until the new unit was completed.

As though there were not enough set-backs, even the fibres division was facing a decline in worldwide pulp and paper trade, its profits boosted only by its decision to raise its stake in Eucalyptus Pulp Mills to just over 20 per cent, thereby enabling it to treat the business as an associate.

With the long-awaited and desperately needed upturn in brick demand failing to materialise anywhere by the end of 1981, Ibstock Johnsen ended the year in bad shape.

Losses in Holland and the US, together with high interest charges and the added aggravation of currency losses - Sterling depreciated by 20 per cent against the Dollar and by eight per cent against the Guilder - almost cancelled out another creditable UK performance, despite a recession now so severe that the kiln was shut down at Roughdales' Eltonhead plant. The 80 redundancies were described as "a bitter blow" by Walker.

The ghastliness of the overall situation was starkly underlined in the year's results. Ibstock Johnsen, having hit a pre-tax profit peak of just over £5m in 1978, could now manage only £175,000 on worldwide turnover of more than £60m. "Avoid

Ibstock!" screamed some of the analysts' newsletters, though others still backed the business as a good, longer-term bet.

As Ibstock Johnsen dragged itself towards the end of a terrible year it received a rare boost to morale in the form of an announcement that it had become the first brick manufacturer to win the Royal Society of Arts Presidential Award for Design Management.

The award represented an acknowledgement of the efforts made by Ibstock to promote the use of high-quality brickwork, embracing its wide product range, its ability to produce special shapes, its marketing strategy and its advisory service for brickwork design.

It was, according to Graham Walker, a source of celebration in the midst of almost unmitigated despondency: "We had filled in the application form on the premise that our design management concept, from boardroom through to sales, was worth just as much as any other industrial design concept.

Prince Philip, The Duke of Edinburgh, presenting Paul Hyde-Thomson with the Royal Society of Arts Presidential Award for Design Management in recognition of the company's successful promotion of brick in architecture.

"The jury were clearly fascinated and came to visit us. We won our category alongside a cutlery maker, a perfume manufacturer and someone who produced cigarette-making equipment."

The chairman took the opportunity for a quick commercial: "I am convinced that our insistence on high quality products and customer service and our concern to look beyond bricks to the finished building and its environment are our best safeguards for the future."

Ten days before Christmas Hyde-Thomson attended a

ceremony at the Royal Society of Arts in London, at which the award was presented to him by H.R.H. The Duke of Edinburgh. There would be few excuses for celebrations in the year ahead.

11

Rock bottom

THE harsh winter snows, fuel shortages and appalling road conditions which heralded the arrival of 1982 did not augur well for what already looked like being a very chilly year.

In the UK a reorganisation of management was to see John Milham, who, as general manager, had spent five years knocking the Cattybrook factory into shape, become production director of Ibstock Building Products. He was joined on the board by Peter Bray, the former sales manager, who was promoted to sales director.

Graham Walker stepped up efforts to extract maximum returns from the domestic businesses in the full knowledge that their performance was again likely to be dragged down by the crises overseas. As one financial columnist put it: "The group's UK showing stands out like a good deed in a naughty world."

There was new promotional material and even a call to employees to urge their families to keep an eye open for possible sales leads and to pass them on. Cash limits were imposed on departments, flexible working hours were introduced and some brick lines were available at significant discounts. Plans were activated for a second brickwork design centre in Birmingham, which was to form the base for a new sales drive in the West

Midlands under David Holmes, the former sales manager at Ibstock who had been appointed sales manager for the West Midlands region. "We had to set up an entirely new sales front and the new design centre was to be its focus. A lot of local merchants saw us as competition and were not amused but the clients quickly appreciated it."

The Birmingham centre would, subsequently, be expanded and followed by others in locations throughout the country, as well as in the US.

But if there was a sense of progress in places like Birmingham, there was a feeling of growing despair in locations like Heteren, Udenhout and Maren. Attempts by the Dutch brick industry to reduce its production more in line with existing and foreseeable demand were not proving sufficiently effective. Ruga Beheer's own indebtedness was still climbing remorselessly and heading for a year-end total of £8m. More heavy trading losses were on the way.

According to Wesseling: "We came to the inevitable conclusion that we had to get out, even if closing all the factories and sacking every employee would cost us millions of guilders. Compared with carrying on with such losses, even that seemed like a good deal."

Graham Walker, who was still spending some of his time in Holland, had come to the same conclusion as his colleagues. "It was clear that the best possible thing for us to do was to get out. The market was still collapsing around our ears and there was no more we could do about it." As the year progressed Ruga was on course for losses of £2.5m on turnover of under £8m; Ibstock Johnsen was on course for an embarrassing retreat.

By the autumn, with US housing starts falling to their lowest level since 1946, Glen-Gery held production to 40 per cent of capacity in order to reduce stocks and raise cash flow. John Kerr was on his way back home to the UK, where he preferred to live, having carried out many of the changes demanded by the recessionary conditions.

His departure left the group board with the dilemma of choosing a replacement from the US or finding a member of the UK team to continue the battle with a loss-making business. Boxall volunteered before the chairman could suggest that he was probably the best person for the job and he at once assumed direct responsibility for the American operations as president.

In retrospect, he believes he should have gone earlier: "We

delayed in getting to grips with the situation. The chairman and I were flying backwards and forwards across the Atlantic, following each other about like a pair of Siamese twins.

"We must have been thoroughly confusing everyone, failing to make it clear who was running what. At a much earlier stage I should have gone to America, leaving Paul with responsibility for the rest of the group's business. As it was there were too many cooks spoiling the broth for too long."

By the time he arrived, announcing that the US was to be his home (with the clear implication that he intended to stay until everything was sorted out the Ibstock way) the American market had hit rock-bottom.

Glen-Gery had 200 million bricks in stock, serious management problems and little confidence in its own future: "The business was on its uppers. Its reputation had been shot to pieces and everyone was laughing at the English. John Kerr had done a lot of the ground work but there was still a great deal to be done."

The new president conspicuously made himself available to staff, arriving each day at head office in his big American car and ready to listen to suggestions and complaints from anyone who had them. He found a myriad of problems, not least a great deal of misinformation within the construction industry about Ibstock's attitude towards sales.

Glen-Gery, in the eyes of too many people, had been painted as the brick producer which had cut out the middle-men, despite the fact that over two-thirds of its product was still being sold through dealers.

Boxall's every move was being closely watched from home. As he set about establishing a new management structure and assessing the quality of the personnel he had, some of his colleagues in Britain began to think that the group had simply bitten off more than it could chew; that no-one could save a situation in which continuing losses seemed inevitable and a sale to another owner appeared impossible.

The combined effect of the group's international difficulties meant that, by October, it was acknowledging the prospect of losses for 1982. The directors doggedly maintained their long tradition of maintaining dividends with an interim payment to shareholders, but few people would have readily placed money on the date of the next payout.

Indeed, the entire future of Ibstock Johnsen looked to be

in doubt and the "Rolls Royce" of the brick industry looking increasingly like an old banger about to be driven off the road.

Though, characteristically, he kept his thoughts to himself, the chairman held himself largely to blame: "There was, by now, just the chance that things could get out of control and that the business would go down.

"In the UK we were doing well but the rest looked appalling, with Holland still haemorrhaging and the US in a mess. In America, we had made the right acquisitions but we had tried to create management for two businesses. We did not have sufficient resources and, on top of everything, the market collapsed on us.

"I had made a mess of it. We had been too bold in purchasing more capacity than we had in the UK. We were having to tell the US that it could not spend a penny more than it took in. It was just a matter of trying to survive. We crawled one step forward and then took six steps back."

Ibstock's dire problems inevitably now attracted the attention of others in the brick industry. In particular, the biggest brick manufacturer of all had been watching very closely.

It had not been so very long since Ibstock had been notching up higher profits that London Brick, the industry's predominant producer. Now, however, the situation looked very different.

Jeremy Rowe, of London Brick, and Hyde-Thomson had talked casually in the past about the possibility of the two businesses getting together but nothing had ever come of their conversations. With Ibstock looking vulnerable and with concern rising about the prospect of a major calamity in the industry, Rowe chose to re-open the issue.

For London Brick there was more than one reason for pursuing the possibility of a takeover. An extensive market research programme had already convinced it that the low cost of fletton bricks in relation to other brick types was no longer as important as it had been in the stringent, post-war days of mass council house building programmes. Instead, there was a definite trend towards the use of higher- quality, higher-cost, higher-margin bricks offering more aesthetic appeal and yet still representing a modest cost element in most construction projects.

With 75 per cent of its customers by now purchasing direct from London Brick, the group had come to the conclusion that it ought to be able to extend its product range by establishing a foothold in the facings market and then expanding it further.

The group had already converted one of its hollow clay block plants to produce quality facing bricks and further similar initiatives were in the pipeline. A deal with Ibstock would represent a huge step along the way to achieving its ambitions.

The shift, no doubt, had been encouraged by the group's own difficulties in its traditional market place. The drop in housing starts, upon which it was largely dependent, had already forced it to close four plants and to cut the workforce from 8,400 to 5,000.

There were further attractions. Rowe in particular cherished a special ambition for his company - that of converting what was already one of the world's leading brickmakers into a major player on the international brick scene. It was now in partnership with Brick and Pipe Industries, of Melbourne, as a major producer in Australia, while Ibstock had established its bridgeheads in Europe and the United States.

Like Blue Circle, London Brick wanted to stick to the product it knew best but believed it could also repeat the formula of building an international business based on its successes in its domestic market. At home the two businesses would complement each other well.

There was an additional factor in the calculations. By now there was genuine concern within the brick industry and within the Department of the Environment about the fate of Ibstock. Ministers were expressing concern about what might happen and London Brick found an implicit welcome at the DOE for the possibility of a merger between the two groups.

The question of a possible reference to the Monopolies Commission was raised but the industrial logic appeared sensible and, though the prospect of yet another industry investigation was hardly a matter for much enthusiasm, the first moves were made.

According to Rowe: "We were not just taking advantage of the market opportunity. If we had been, we would simply have launched an outright bid. We wanted an agreed deal in which both sides believed there were positive benefits."

Even so, London Brick had invited Ibstock to the negotiating table at a time when it was at its most vulnerable. The two companies and their advisers - Kleinwort Benson for

Ibstock and Morgan Grenfell for London Brick - sat down to talk. The stage was set for negotiations which could transform the structure of the UK brick sector.

Ten days before Christmas the London Stock Exchange announced that shares in Ibstock Johnsen had been temporarily suspended at 81p - the highest level of the year and a price which valued the business at nearly £23m. The decision at once gave rise to a flood of speculation about the next step. Though a bid appeared to be the obvious reason, the favoured bidders were not London Brick but Hanson Trust, the owners of Butterley Brick and, with 23 per cent of the non-fletton market, a market share slightly higher than that of Ibstock.

An earlier attempt to raise Hanson's market share still further, via the acquisition of G.H. Downing, the Staffordshire brick producer, had failed. Downing had ended up in the arms of Steetley, the building materials and heat-resistant products group which now had a share of the non-fletton market similar to that of Hanson.

In response to press inquiries Hanson said it was company policy not to comment on rumours while Colin Corness said Redland was not the cause of the share suspension. There was a short-lived silence from London Brick.

The following morning the mystery was unravelled with the public unveiling of London Brick's £27m agreed cash-and-shares offer for Ibstock Johnsen. Ibstock's directors, holding nearly three per cent of the equity, were supporting the deal and recommending it to other shareholders. Hyde-Thomson reflects: "In the final analysis, we decided to go along with London Brick for safety."

The terms were not considered to be overly-generous in the City but most pundits accepted that, given Ibstock's problems, they would probably prove sufficiently attractive to its shareholders.

In a press statement London Brick described both companies as eminent in their respective but different brick markets. It claimed that, in order to ensure the industry continued to receive the same high and individual standard of service, the two groups' operations would be kept quite separate, although both would have the benefit of London Brick's research facilities and the increased resources and expertise resulting from the marriage.

The statement said that the creation of the new group, in

an industry in which Britain was traditionally a leader in technology, would enable a strong overseas presence to be maintained and further developed. Apart from the US, Europe and Australia, London Brick made it clear that it also had its eyes on the developing world. A merger, it added, would greatly enhance the growth and development of the two companies.

Under the terms agreed, Hyde-Thomson, Boxall and Walker would join the board of London Brick, retaining their existing responsibilities with Ibstock. Hyde-Thomson would also become a non-executive deputy chairman of London Brick.

On Christmas Eve the formal offer document was published. It revealed the true depth of Ibstock's catalogue of problems. The board disclosed that the group was heading for a loss in 1982 of about £1.5m - it turned out at £1.4m - a figure again exacerbated by exchange losses and by heavy group borrowings which could not quickly be reduced. More losses in the US and Holland were expected in 1983.

London Brick, however, had performed well despite the difficulties in the market place and was heading for 1982 pre-tax profits of at least £15m. Hyde-Thomson told his shareholders: "London Brick is a fine company, being one of the leading brickmakers in the world. It has shown a good increase in profits over the last two years, its prospects appear good and it is in a strong financial position."

He pledged that Ibstock would retain its separate identity and that its customers would continue to receive the same high standards of service to which they had become accustomed. It was, he stressed, a merger of complementary interests in which customers and employees would benefit.

As for the possibility of another probe by the Monopolies and Mergers Commission, the defence was already in place. London Brick now had about 39 per cent of the national brick market - down from 45 per cent at the time of the 1976 investigation - and Ibstock around seven per cent, against 21 per cent of the market for facing bricks.

The combination of the two companies' market shares was, therefore, little different from that which London Brick had held on its own when it was last put under the microscope.

But if the deal looked straightforward enough and attractive to the respective boards of the two soon-to-be-wed partners, their feelings were by no means universally shared.

The news had come out of the blue to Ibstock's employees,

many of whom were not as enthusiastic as the architects of the deal. Jack Watton, a former group administration manager and, by the time of the London Brick bid, general manager at Himley, recalls the deep disquiet shared by many of his colleagues: "There was what can only be described as a fairly serious rebellion. Many of us did not understand the chairman's logic in attempting such a move.

"People at the centre were very unhappy, believing that their jobs were on the line. There was also a general feeling that we were being sold off on the cheap. None of us liked it and many were quite ready to consider packing up and leaving."

A principal source of concern centred on what were perceived as the cultural differences between the two groups. There were few doubts about Ibstock's ability to work alongside London Brick personnel but much greater reservations about the nature of London Brick's product, which was simply regarded as inferior.

Such were the fears surrounding the deal that a meeting of senior managers was called - with Hyde-Thomson and Boxall noticeably off the invitation list - to express united opposition to the move. According to Jack Watton: "We left Graham Walker in no doubt that we were totally against it and that we were, in any case, worth a damned site more than had been offered. He was naturally disappointed but had no choice but to report back with our opinions."

Walker had no such doubts, although he well remembers the unease of the managers: "They made their feelings quite clear. I was set to join the London Brick board but, even without that personal consideration, I could see all the advantages of selling our bricks through a much larger organisation, without it diluting Ibstock's own standing. It could have been a great opportunity."

The saga however, had several more twists to it. With 1983 only 13 days old and, as Lord Cockfield, the Trade Secretary, still deliberated on whether or not to refer the merger to the Monopolies and Mergers Commission, the orderly progression towards amicable merger was rudely stopped in its tracks.

Colin Corness, the chairman of Redland, the Reigate-based building materials group, had already seen Ibstock's chairman to put his own alternative proposals. Only weeks before Corness had spent £43m on acquiring a Texas-based limestone quarrying operation and now he was prepared to put £34.7m in cash or shares on the table to win control of Ibstock Johnsen.

Redland, with about 15 per cent of the non-fletton market already under its corporate belt, announced its plan. It hailed the proposal as an opportunity to weld together a nationwide business with strong traditions both of high standards of customer service and of product innovation. Together they would "form a significant counter-force" to London Brick's dominant market position.

Claiming a Redland-Ibstock merger would offer a "better business fit," Redland emphasised that, while its own brick-making plants were principally located in the south east of England, Ibstock was primarily in the Midlands and the north west.

There were further similarities. In Holland Redland had already forged a partnership with Verenigde Bedrijven Bredero to manufacture concrete roof tiles. It had also recently purchased none other than Delta Baksteen, the brick company over which Ibstock's chairman had originally cast an acquisitive eye.

Redland, which was also involved in the Dutch brick industry's combined attempts to solve its over-capacity crisis, said that the amalgamation of its interests in Holland with those of Ibstock would create a major force in an important European market.

The geographical connections went further. In the US Redland had proved its intentions by its most recent acquisition and it expressed confidence that recent evidence of a recovery in US construction activity would lead to a sharp improvement in Ibstock's poor state of health.

Its offer, said Corness, was "manifestly more attractive" than that of London Brick. Hyde-Thomson, who would join Redland's board and become chairman of the enlarged group's international brick division, told Ibstock shareholders to take no action in respect of London Brick's bid, which had so far been accepted by shareholders representing eight per cent of Ibstock equity.

Redland's surprise emergence helped confirm its reputation as something of a dark horse in City circles. Less than a year earlier, it had popped up as the unexpected bidder for another UK group and had recently given the impression that it was far too busy with its new US purchase to think of any other deals.

According to the Financial Times: "Now it has emerged from the shadows to spoil the happy marriage which London Brick and Ibstock have been planning for themselves."

News of the alternative bid pushed up Ibstock shares to a point at which the group was valued at just over £30m. "Redland Barge in on Ibstock Brick Marriage" ran one headline. It had certainly set the cat among the corporate pigeons.

12

Turning point

FIVE days after Redland had decided to enter the battle for ownership of Ibstock Johnsen, London Brick announced that it was extending by three weeks, rather than improving, its offer which had so far been accepted in respect of nearly 15 per cent of the issued equity. Shareholders had until February to accept Redland's alternative bid.

The announcement was accompanied by an assurance that there would be no new initiative from the group until Lord Cockfield made it clear that the bid would not be referred to the Mergers and Monopolies Commission. The Commission had already prepared its report on London Brick's offer but had been forced to withdraw and reconsider the situation in view of Redland's intervention.

Hyde-Thomson repeated his advice to shareholders to take no action in respect of either offer and said that the extraordinary general meeting - scheduled for January 17 and originally expected to endorse the merger with London Brick - was being postponed for one month. At the end of January the tension was broken when Lord Cockfield announced, somewhat reluctantly, that both bids would need to be investigated. Ibstock didn't know it but it would prove to be a liferaft decision for the embattled company.

Both offers now lapsed. Michael Wright, London Brick's deputy chairman, said its original offer was "no longer a valid piece of paper" and Hyde-Thomson acknowledged that it was likely to be several months before any conclusions were reached. In the meantime, he stressed, Ibstock was in "good heart" and was continuing to pursue the steps necessary to restore it to profits.

One such step was only a few weeks away.

In Holland the position had not improved, with the major brick manufacturers still failing to reach agreement on a collective response to their problems.

Graham Walker was by now sounding out the chances of finding a customer for its Dutch business. The prospects looked slim, given the almost universally shared opinion that the continuing outlook for the brick industry remained bleak.

Dirk Wesseling, who would retire in early 1984, believed the recession would last at least five years, making impossible the prospect of a decent revival for Ibstock's operations. But he found one or two brickmakers who were more optimistic and none more so than a company called Redland-Braas-Bredero Europa, the joint venture tile-making business which Redland half-owned.

Walker spent a week showing the potential owners around the six factories, explaining everything through interpreters but knowing full well they understood everything he said.

At the same time he was spelling out to a loyal workforce how things had been going from bad to worse: "One of the worst moments in my career was having to stand up in front of 150 men to tell them they had no jobs. Ibstock had told them for years that they were safe with us. It was the sort of situation which would have been bad enough at home but it just felt so much worse in another country."

Vendor and purchaser spent hours in a smoke-filled room thrashing out an acceptable deal. Once the terms were agreed the transaction itself was quickly completed. A statement from Lutterworth House said that Ibstock had solved its problems in Holland by selling out to the Redland joint venture for £1.2m cash.

Hyde-Thomson disclosed that, following an interim assets write-off of just under £2m on the Dutch operations, there would be a further write-off of £7.5m. In 1982, he revealed, Holland had recorded trading losses of around £2.3m. The chairman expressed regret at the decision but said the group's financial position would now be much stronger.

The announcement of the deal, though of considerable relief to Ibstock, was not well received at London Brick's York Gate headquarters on the edge of Regents Park in London. Having agreed a friendly bid with Ibstock the board was surprised that it had not been kept in touch with such a major development.

When the sale agreement was concluded Hyde-Thomson telephoned Rowe to pass on the news. The London Brick chairman says it was the point at which he should have begun to wonder whether Ibstock's enthusiasm for a merger might have started to cool.

"Perhaps the alarm bells should have started ringing. It was obviously the correct thing for Ibstock to do, but the sale meant their business was considerably less exposed. They were under no obligation of any kind to consult us on the Redland deal but we were in the process of making our mutual representations to the Monopolies Commission, so it would have helped us if we had known."

The withdrawal from Holland - finally leaving Wanlin as the group's only toehold within continental Europe - was the cause for undisguised relief within Ibstock, though its failure to overcome the problems, which had dogged the acquisition from its earliest days, was also the source of deep disappointment. The decision was to prove an important psychological and financial turning point within the group.

At the start of April Redland made a surprise announcement. It had decided not to pursue its attempt to win control of Ibstock irrespective of the outcome of the Monopolies and Mergers Commission's findings.

Colin Corness believed that Ibstock's trading position was improving, which would probably force it to raise the terms of its original offer, while it was far from certain that clearance for any such takeover would be forthcoming, thereby raising the possibility of wasting months of management time on an initiative which could never be fulfilled.

Suspicions harboured in some circles that Redland had, in any case, only mounted a counter-bid in an attempt to spoil a neatly arranged merger - which would have presented its own brick interests with increased competition - were hardly allayed when the predator suddenly withdrew.

The decision provoked a surprisingly upbeat reaction from Hyde-Thomson, who sounded more confident about the future than he had done at any time during the past difficult months. He told the newspapers: "Our fortunes have changed. We do not need suitors. We have disposed of our Dutch company, which was a major headache, and now everything looks rather different."

Different it certainly was. With Holland gone, the UK business was recording a substantial increase in profits on the back of fatter order books. Big reductions in interest rates were stimulating another upsurge in construction, particularly in the private housing sector, where starts were running one third ahead on a year earlier. Losses had continued in the US but there were some signs of an improvement in market conditions.

In July, as Mrs. Thatcher settled in to her second term as Prime Minister, Ibstock's chairman wrote to shareholders telling them that the Mergers and Monopolies Commission had now submitted their report to the Trade and Industry Secretary and that publication was expected shortly. On the group's performance he said that the group was likely to report pre-tax profits of around £1.5m for the first half of the year, almost a complete reversal of the position in the same period 12 months earlier.

He reported that favourable market factors were strengthening the group's businesses both in the UK and the US and disclosed that there were plans to raise UK brick production by up to 20 per cent over the following three years. There was now a strong cash flow, which would be used to eat into borrowings over the next 18 months. The omission of any reference to the continuing possibility of a merger with London Brick was, however, perhaps the most significant element of his statement.

During the second week of August the long-awaited findings of the Commission were published. It gave the green light to a merger plan which had first emerged eight months earlier.

The Commission, headed by Sir Godfray Le Quesne, concluded that the acquisition of Ibstock by London Brick would not affect competition in the supply of common bricks. It also concluded that the market for fletton facing bricks, as produced

Some of the many special shaped bricks made by Ibstock to satisfy the individual needs of customers.

Making brick beautiful. Decorative and hand-made products designed to provide an extra dimension to brick's appeal.

Award-winning brick. Computers were used in the design of Centre Culturel in Marche-en-Famenne to provide one of Belgium's newest cultural centres with the highest quality acoustics, involving the extensive use of complex patterns of Ibstock brick from its Belgium factory. The building won the Award for Theatre Design at the Prague International Festival.

Close to home. A novel application for Ibstock brick, incorporated in the City of Leicester's coat of arms outside the Town Hall.

by London Brick, and non-fletton facing bricks, were largely separate. The merger, it believed, would not have any appreciable impact on competition in either market.

The Commission added: "On consideration of all arguments, and of the past record of London Brick's conduct as total monopolist of the supply of fletton bricks, we do not feel able to conclude that the merged company may be expected to prejudice the public interest by exploitation of its market power."

The report revealed that, in London Brick's opinion, Ibstock faced an uncertain future as an independent company, given its serious overseas problems. Ibstock, however, had told the Commission that its circumstances had changed considerably since first agreeing to the merger.

The group had emphasised that it no longer saw itself in need of rescue and its future attitude towards marriage with London Brick would depend upon a number of factors, particularly the price and the opportunities for Ibstock to contribute to the management of the merged business.

On release of the Commission's findings the reaction from the two participants sowed a certain amount of confusion in financial circles. Jeremy Rowe welcomed the report by claiming "the way is now open for London Brick to make a major incursion into the non-fletton market."

But he added, pointedly: "Ibstock is but one method of approach." Also under consideration, he hinted, was further investment in greenfield sites as well as the possibility of offers for small regional non-fletton manufacturers. To some observers the remarks were seen as an attempt to deliberately suppress Ibstock's value as a prelude to another bid.

Among all the new factors to be taken into account, none was more important than the cost of any renewed merger package. Such had been the recovery in Ibstock's trading record and in its future prospects that its strengthened share price meant London Brick would now have to consider a bid worth £44m for a business which, eight months previously, Ibstock itself believed had been fairly valued at £27m.

Takeover Panel rules gave London Brick, holding four per cent of Ibstock equity, three weeks to decide whether or not to relaunch a fresh bid.

From Ibstock came a carefully-worded reaction. Hyde-Thomson poured on the optimism, predicting record profits for 1983 and claiming that even better days lay ahead.

The chairman gave an assurance that, if London Brick sought to re-open bid discussions, Ibstock would consider the approach. But he made it clear that the directors would not recommend any offer unless the terms and conditions were "very substantially" better than those originally put on the table by London Brick or Redland.

Despite its stand Ibstock could not be sure that London Brick's departure would leave it in the clear. There was considerable concern over rumours that none other than Hanson Trust had, in recent weeks, built up a near-five per cent holding in Ibstock. There was a possibility that it might revive its old ambition to own the business when the dust had settled. The message to London Brick could not have been clearer. With the clock ticking away the directors met to consider their options. After lengthy talks Morgan Grenfell were despatched by London Brick, on Friday, August 19, to see Ibstock's advisers at Kleinwort Benson.

Britain's largest brickmaker was still intent upon winning Ibstock and Morgan Grenfell spelled out the terms of a new offer. London Brick would, the merchant bank suggested, be prepared to exchange two of its own ordinary shares for every ordinary share in Ibstock. By the Monday London Brick - whose own financial performance was now rapidly improving - had added a cash element of "at least 15p" to the package. It was all conditional upon a recommendation of acceptance from the Ibstock board, additional confirmation that pre-tax profits in 1983 would exceed £6m - a figure which had not been mentioned in Ibstock's forecasts of a record year - and assurances on how the group intended to tackle its continuing problems in the US.

The bid valued Ibstock at £51.7m - nearly twice the value first placed on the company in the previous December and 40 per cent above the Redland offer. The chairman, Richard Boxall and Graham Walker would, as originally planned, join London Brick's board.

But by now Ibstock was not interested. As the year had progressed, so its confidence and its determination to remain independent had grown. Kleinworts said that the offer was not acceptable to their clients and, on the evening of August 23, rejected on behalf of Ibstock the idea of any more talks.

The following morning London Brick announced that, in the absence of an Ibstock recommendation, it would proceed no further. Jeremy Rowe explained: "We have gone as high with our new offer as we thought was prudent. We're going to call it a day."

Michael Wright said the possibility of a contested bid had never been on the cards: "For this to have worked properly, there would have to be total co-operation between the two companies. In our view, it was not desirable to get into a contested situation."

Hyde-Thomson responded: "We prefer to remain independent and it looks as though we may be allowed to." In a statement to Ibstock shareholders, by now used to the thrills and spills of takeover fever, he repeated the view that London Brick's offer, however much improved, was not acceptable.

He added: "In coming to this conclusion, we have taken into account the radical change in the company's position since the end of last year and the significantly improved outlook for this year and beyond. Against this background, your board believes that shareholders' interests are best met by Ibstock Johnsen remaining independent and shareholders benefiting directly from our future, major growth."

It was the end of a traumatic chapter in Ibstock's history, a period which the chairman would later describe as the most difficult it had ever encountered. Less than a year before the group's problems, momentarily at least, appeared almost intractable and the only formula for survival appeared to lie in a marriage with a stronger organisation.

It was a remedy which the board was ready to implement in order to keep the business alive but it would have spelled the end of the independence which Ibstock had so proudly maintained. Now the tide had turned and the future looked secure.

Whatever Redland's motives may have been for entering the fray, the Monopolies and Mergers Commission investigation that it helped provoke had bought Ibstock valuable time. It had fought off two tough adversaries and was now free to pursue its own strategy for revival.

There was deep disappointment at London Brick and particularly for Jeremy Rowe: "Throughout, Ibstock may have been more lukewarm than we were about the strategy we had set out. I might have been a little too romantic about creating a worldwide organisation primarily dedicated to bricks, although Paul also appeared enthusiastic about the idea. I think a wonderful opportunity was lost. The whole episode was perhaps, in the final analysis, rather sad."

The repercussions of the bid for Ibstock were not quite

over, however. The conclusions of the Commission report had encouraged London Brick to believe that the group itself would be safe from corporate attack. The report made it clear that its acceptance of the industrial logic of a London Brick-Ibstock deal did not in any sense provide tacit approval for any other linkings between major brick suppliers and other conglomerates.

But London Brick was wrong. Almost at once, Hanson Trust - never far from the scene of the action - pounced on Britain's biggest brickmaker. According to Tony Alexander, a Hanson director: "By agreeing to the Ibstock-London Brick deal, the investigation opened the door to us, as owners of Butterley, to go for the predator in the earlier bid. It did us a big favour. We had the financial capacity to buy London Brick and we had no problems with the Mergers and Monopolies Commission."

Hanson struck in December 1983. It was a short but bloody battle, with Rowe taking some comfort from the fact that Hanson, for the first time in its history, was forced to raise its price on two occasions in order to capture the prize. "At the time I was more concerned for the future of our employees but our shareholders had an absolute bonanza," recalls Rowe with some consolatory pleasure.

Within Ibstock attention had returned to its own, still numerous, problems. By October the chairman had been able to report half-time profits marginally up on the forecast made on the eve of publication of the Mergers and Monopolies Commission.

The UK brick market, yet again, had supported the rest of the group's operations, with trading profits reaching over £5m. As part of its continuing investment programme the group was now well advanced with the commissioning at plants across the country of modern kilns and the implementation of the latest manufacturing technology.

New products were also being added to the range, with Aldridge, Himley and Nostell all developing new lines and introducing them onto the market.

In November Ian Maclellan, who had joined Ibstock more than four years earlier as financial controller, joined the board as finance director. His first months in the hot seat brought much better news.

In the second half of 1983, during which Ibstock purchased the remaining equity in the loss-making Crusader Board and Converters, the group's health had further improved.

Turnover rose in Britain and the US to end the year on £89m, while profits hit £6.5m, the highest ever.

It was a figure which would comfortably have met the bid pre-condition set by London Brick, although it did not overly impress a stock market which was now becoming used to dramatic increases in profits for building materials companies. Ibstock shares, which had enjoyed the run of their life during 1983, slipped back.

In the US, where exchange rate losses tipped the business slightly further into the red, the last months of the year brought the first signs of a recovery in Glen-Gery's primary market areas, with all types of construction activity beginning to pick up. As a result brick shipments over the year had climbed out of the 1982 trough to reach 290 million, with total sales income rising by about 20 per cent.

Richard Boxall was busy re-activating plant and pushing for improved quality, better cost control and a wider, more comprehensive product range. Customers had been alienated because of Glen-Gery's inability to match its stocks to their requirements, while its relationships with dealers - which had remained a much more important element in the business than had been originally envisaged - had in many cases fallen apart.

Boxall's priority was to install a new management structure intended to shorten lines of communication and, with so many factories, sales offices and representatives, to emphasise the importance of making decisions where they should be made. A highly-centralised management did not provide the solution.

The president established three corporate divisions, each to be run by a general manager who, in turn, delegated to plant and sales managers. The three divisions, to be set up during 1984, covered the north-east, the mid-west and the south-east and were to be run by managers recruited from outside the brick industry.

Bob Beverforden, a former vice-president of Clarke Chemical Corporation, who would eventually replace Boxall as president, took the mid-west. Ben Riggs, a former US Navy pilot with long experience in the construction sector, was appointed for the north-east. The south-east went to Bill Peckham, a New Yorker who had been involved with the construction business throughout his career.

The group's 11 sales regions remained in place and more salesmen were recruited and trained, with the emphasis placed on the mid-west and south-east, where prospects for more business seemed brightest. Taking a leaf out of the Ibstock book in the UK, Glen-Gery had also opened its first brickwork design centre in downtown Baltimore. In a well-received gesture of goodwill Boxall presented the City with 8,000 paving bricks for use in the imaginative reconstruction of Baltimore's old harbour front.

The concept of a brickmaker, rather than a dealer, opening a design centre was as revolutionary in the US as it had been in the UK. The intention was to keep designers abreast of the latest brick technology. Technical support services, such as a comprehensive brick reference library, design equipment, brick sample system and conference and audio-visual facilities, were also provided.

In addition on-site staff specialists in structural engineering and architectural design would be available to provide guidance on brickwork application from the initial stages of design. Combined with a programme of technical seminars for designers and users of brick, the new design centre was not only intended to enhance Glen-Gery's own battered reputation but to promote further the imaginative and attractive use of brick. Other centres would soon follow in Washington, New York and Philadelphia.

The US business was still some way from profitability but there was a new-found sense of purpose and a fresh confidence that the worst was finally over. From the other side of the Atlantic there was much relief that Ibstock's home market performance was unlikely to be over-shadowed for much longer by events more than three thousand miles away.

13

A new momentum

IF IBSTOCK Johnsen had been put through the mill by recent events, it was now poised to enjoy a period of unparallelled growth and prosperity. As so often in the past, the weather seemed to set the business barometer for the year and 1984 got off to a very mild start.

As Philip Ling, group managing director of London and Midland Industrial, joined the board in a non-executive capacity and Pat Holmes prepared to step down after 20 years as a director, Ibstock's revival gathered pace.

In the UK, where the business was now dependant on the housing market for less than half its sales, further design centres would open in Cambridge and Glasgow.

During the year, in which Ibstock actively supported the Royal Institute of British Architects' Festival of Architecture, nearly all plants commissioned new kiln capacity, a move followed by most other brickmakers.

Efforts were stepped up to widen the group's facing brick range. New textures, colours and shapes were introduced to the market, with a particular emphasis being placed on specials. Rising demand for decorative bricks and paving bricks, in particular, led to more new lines and higher output.

By mid-year the building products business in Ibstock's domestic market had achieved sharply increased trading profits of £7m resulting from higher margins on slightly lower sales. The takeover of London Brick by Hanson had been followed almost at once by substantial price increases for fletton bricks - in central London they rose by up to one-fifth - thereby encouraging other producers to follow suit.

The fibres division, still recovering from one of its worst-ever trading periods, also turned in a half-way profit, helped by hardening world dollar prices for woodpulp and favourable exchange rates. In the US, however, another six-month trading loss was turned in. Boxall bit the bullet even harder with a decision to shut down several of its manufacturing plants in order to reduce a heavily under-utilised annual capacity of 580 million bricks.

The plan was to leave the business on full production at around 450 million bricks and the first casualties were the Watsontown, Morral and Manor plants, the closure of which would lead to a £4.6m write-down in book values. Because of growing difficulties in obtaining raw material supplies, the former Marion plant at Brazil, Indiania, would eventually also close.

"We did not want to be like our US competitors, who were used to running flat out when necessary and then closing down and laying off when the bad times arrived. I did not want us to run that way, so I trimmed capacity to match achievable levels of sales. At the plants we retained we worked damned hard to raise output," Boxall recalls.

By the second half of 1984 the US operations were finally recording profits, as were all other sections of the business - a rare phenomenon since the group had first set foot abroad.

In Britain the industry as a whole, in the shape of the Brick Development Association, had embarked on a fresh sales initiative intended to boost further the use of brick, a move partially stimulated by a worrying fall in the rate of new housing work. Much of the responsibility for the new offensive lay with Graham Walker, who had enthusiastically taken on the chairmanship of the Association and been handed the task of formulating a fresh marketing strategy for its members.

The BDA, which by now represented 95 per cent of UK brick capacity, launched a £600,000 advertising campaign aimed primarily at stepping up sales in higher-margin markets other than housing - a philosophy in which Ibstock Johnsen had already led the way. With a slogan deliberately reminiscent of Tony Cadman's original campaign, the message was spelled out on posters across the country: "Brick Keeps Britain Beautiful."

As the year closed Ibstock stepped back into the acquisition market, though it was a modest step compared with some of the purchases which had preceded the battle for its own independence. Three weeks before Christmas it agreed to pay £2.5m, by way of a vendor placing, for Coalmore Refractories (Horsehay), a privately-owned manufacturer of specialist clay products with useful clay reserves.

Firebricks had been made at Horsehay since the mid-1700s, supplying the new furnaces being built all over the Ironbridge area as the industrial revolution got underway.

The clay deposits were the same which, more than 200 years earlier, had made possible the foundation of the world-famous Caughley porcelain factory, at one time owned by the equally known and admired Coalport porcelain company, which was located nearby.

The business, renamed Ibstock Brick Telford, made little profit but it gave its new owner the opportunity to install plant which would give it a presence in the pressed paving brick market. A greenfield site development would have needed twice the £600,000 investment entailed in the new plant and the cost of the purchase was to be significantly reduced by the sale of surplus agricultural land. David Holmes, as regional sales manager for the West Midlands, was closely involved in the preparation for the launch of the new product line.

"We got the new pavers off the ground, only to be faced with problems with the machinery, difficulties with the raw material and unacceptable costings. It was decided to switch to brick production, although by this time we had attracted a considerable number of paver orders. It was a potentially embarrassing situation but we got out of it without losing too much face."

Ibstock's performance in 1984 lived up to all expectations. When the final figures were disclosed the extent of its recovery was clear. During the year it had managed to push up pre-tax profits to £12.4m., almost double the level achieved in the previous 12 months.

On every front the business had made impressive advances. Total turnover had risen by 25 per cent to £110m, with the UK and US businesses taking an almost equal share of the cake. Ibstock brick plants despatched 653 million bricks to their customers. The fibres division also hit the jackpot with trading profits, on the back of soaring pulp prices, reaching in excess of £2m.

The group balance sheet had strengthened, borrowings had been contained and earnings per share leaped by 85 per cent, resulting in a 45 per cent rise in the total dividend payout.

The US turnround was particularly heartening. There was still a year-end loss of less than $1m, reflecting the poor start to the year, but profits had now been restored and looked set to rise.

Boxall's task had not been entirely comprised of organising retrenchment and chasing cost-savings. He had also put in hand a $1.5m project to begin hand-made brick production at Glen-Gery's York, Pennsylvania, plant, utilising much of the equipment from the Manor unit. Handmade bricks were already being produced at New Oxford and the York facility provided an additional annual capacity of 18 million units.

At the Capitol plant at Manassas, near Washington, the latest brick press from Holland was being installed to enable the manufacture of moulded bricks. Both product lines were increasingly popular in Glen-Gery's local markets, as well as further afield in the US.

The beginning of 1985, ushered in by a severe winter and the approaching first anniversary of the miners' strike, brought a disposal and another addition to the Ibstock Johnsen stable in the UK.

In February the group finally parted company with Crusader Board and Converters, where losses had finally been stopped but where further development was ruled out. But in April, as the group disclosed its final results for 1984, it announced the acquisition of H.F. Warner, a long-established, Berkshire-based manufacturer of "rustic look" clay roofing tiles, a market in which Ibstock was keen to participate. The price was £5.5m, largely satisfied by a vendor placing, with the £1m balance in cash. The purchase represented Ibstock's first move into clay roof tiles in the UK and, although a relatively small purchase, the Warners acquisition was seen as potentially the start of something more ambitious. The new owners believed they could not only double Warner's annual output of five million tiles but extend production to other plants where suitable clay reserves existed.

But the deal did not indicate a resumption of the group's appetite for corporate takeovers. After its recent traumas the emphasis had changed to consolidation. In the UK a management structure which had become stretched by continuous organic growth and acquisition was in the process of being tightened and strengthened. A major company-wide exercise aimed at improving productivity was also undertaken with the help of outside consultants.

The nationwide network of design centres was completed with further openings in Bristol and Leeds. As part of Ibstock's mission to maintain its educational contribution to the industry it resumed its co-operation with the Royal Institute of British Architects to sponsor an architectural exhibition displaying the works of younger designers.

Entitled "40 Under Forty," the travelling exhibition provided a showcase for 40 architects under the age of 40 to provide an insight into their own talents and to the latest trends in construction design. The idea had originated back in the 1940s in New York - where Ibstock's latest design centre was being opened - and it had been resurrected in the mid-1960s. Now the RIBA wanted to try it again and Ibstock Johnsen was eager to help.

A panel of judges assessed the merits of 117 entries and whittled them down to provide an exhibition embracing the widest range of design projects from individual houses to major office and industrial complexes. Premiered at RIBA headquarters, the exhibition then moved to Ibstock's design centres around the UK where it was seen by more than 18,000 designers.

The following year, in which the US business co-sponsored a memorial lecture on architecture and an exhibition of architectural drawings, "40 Under Forty" went on the road to Washington, New York, Philadelphia, Baltimore and Boston to help raise public awareness of brick and of Glen-Gery.

The US business was, during 1985, finally beginning to produce the type of results which had proved doggedly elusive ever since its acquisition. Although there would be continuing reminders of earlier traumas, like the final closure of the Brazil plant and a further assets write-down of £4.9m, the business was now looking decidedly upbeat and heading into the black.

Glen-Gery was on course for a creditable turnround from

the previous year, reporting a trading profit of just over £1m - though margins at only two per cent were hardly the sort of returns which had been envisaged at the time Ibstock had first crossed the Atlantic. In the UK, during 1985, they were running at 26 per cent. Glen-Gery's turnover rose sharply to $80m, reflecting the deepening market penetration which was being achieved.

The business also took a pride in demonstrating that its ingenuity extended beyond the range of products it could offer its customers. It also had some ideas up its sleeve when it came to manufacturing as well as marketing.

At its Bigler, Pennsylvania, plant, for example, the need to remain competitive had intensified the search for cost-effective production techniques and attention had focused on finding a less expensive fuel than natural gas.

Given that Bigler stood in the heart of a region characterised by vast tracts of hardwood forest, sawdust seemed an obvious choice, especially as it was already being used successfully by many brick plants in the southern part of the country. A $1.5m conversion scheme, paid for in two years by lower production costs, was agreed and started. Bigler was set to become what it liked to describe as Glen-Gery's "flagship sawdust firing plant."

To complete the picture Bigler also introduced a new brick containing an element of sawdust. The lighter weight brick, which met all other required specifications, meant larger truck consignments and provided Glen-Gery customers with another attractive alternative.

The US business was also about to take advantage of an unexpected opportunity which was simply too good to miss. In the Spring of 1985 Richard Hanley of Hanley Brick, based at Summerville near Pittsburgh, Pennsylvania, telephoned Hyde-Thomson, asking if Glen-Gery was interested in buying the business.

Hanley was a major force in the north-east market, having been established about as long as Glen-Gery and with an excellent reputation. Its plant manufactured very high quality architectural facing bricks, providing a useful complement to Glen-Gery's own widening range.

The Summerville complex also manufactured paving materials, chemical resistant bricks and glazed bricks, which were currently enjoying something of a renaissance among specifiers. Production capacity stood at 50 million bricks a year.

By the summer Glen-Gery had taken a good look at the Hanley operation and negotiations for its purchase began in the autumn. The deal would be concluded in early 1986 at a cost to Glen-Gery of just over $5m. It was a strategically intelligent purchase, which also proved psychologically important to a business again beginning to believe in itself. As one financial columnist put it: "It looks as though the American nut has finally been cracked."

With a splendid touch of irony the brightening outlook in the US throughout 1985 - where turnover for the first time exceeded that in the UK - was not being repeated at home. The combination of a terrible winter and the final death throes of the miners' strike had hit production at several plants. The early lost ground was not to be made up.

Manufacturers' deliveries fell by five per cent and by the end of 1985 the industry as a whole confronted facing brick stocks up by two-thirds on a year earlier, equivalent to around two months' output. Ibstock could not escape the trend and, although it maintained market share, margins came under severe pressure.

As a result total group pre-tax profits fell back to £11.4m on turnover of £116m. Total brick deliveries by all the group's businesses reached 703 million.

Apart from Warners there were to be no further acquisitions in the UK during the year, although Graham Walker made it clear that the group remained intent upon making strategic investments in both new and existing plant. The year saw continuing and heavy capital investment at a number of UK plants; there were new additions to the product range at Leicester, output was raised at Cattybrook and special shape facilities were installed at Nostell. A new range of moulded products was in the pipeline at Himley and there was further investment at the Hudson factories.

The fibres business, in the meantime, which had never expected to repeat its 1984 performance, remained in profit. But it found itself struggling in chaotic international trading conditions brought about by over-production of pulp, volatile exchange rates and a new EEC price directive forbidding the use of the US dollar as the sole currency for trading pulp.

The next 12 months were to see Ibstock's momentum gather pace across all areas of its business, reflected in rising sales and higher profits and reinforced by continuing efforts to strengthen management.

For once every area of activity moved ahead and, mid-year, profits were running a third up on 1985. High levels of construction output provided the platform for a further improvement in performance within the US, which was heading for a record-breaking year.

American brick sales reached a new peak - to account for 60 per cent of the 765 million despatched throughout the group - and output was also at a new high. Cost control procedures were, at the same time, becoming increasingly effective and, with selling prices moving sharply higher, the record of poor margins began to improve. The end result was a profit of more than £5m.

Glen-Gery began to expand its production distribution by extending its sales effort into the southern and western markets of the US. For the first time brick shipments went as far afield as Texas, Florida and California.

There were new products as well as new markets. Apart from the additional lines provided by Hanley, Glen-Gery began marketing an interlocking brick wall coping system and a high-quality Portland cement lime mortar. A programme of product rationalisation was also instituted, ensuring that production of each brick type was assigned to the most suitable plant, thereby improving costs, quality and availability.

Among the contracts won during 1986, one in particular helped underline Glen-Gery's newly-emerging status as a materials producer whose contribution towards construction did not stop with the delivery of its bricks. Early in the year the company was approached by the Brick Institute of America and asked if it would help with the renovation of buildings on Ellis Island in New York Harbour.

Between 1912 and 1954 more than 16 million immigrants had passed through Ellis Island where they stepped on to American soil for the first time. The 23-acre island and the 30 buildings upon it were now part of the Statue of Liberty national monument and, together, they held a very special place in the hearts of Americans.

The task now was to breathe new life into buildings which had become part of the nation's heritage and Glen-Gery was called in to donate new bricks which would match those which had been originally used.

With up to 15 varieties of brick included in some of the

buildings the challenge was a complex one but Glen-Gery was glad to make a contribution which would, in the words of the BIA, "show the significance of brick's role in the building of America." Ibstock found its involvement not only flattering but, for a business now described by its president as the "premier brickmaker in the US," it was an excellent promotional exercise.

The encouraging picture established in the US - where one commentator said Glen-Gery had "spent a fortune on teaching New England to love brick," was also being reflected in Ibstock's domestic markets. At home the drive for increased market share, better efficiency, higher output and lower costs was no less intense. There was no let up, either, in Ibstock's marketing drive, still the key to its success in fending off competition from within an increasingly sophisticated brick facings market and from makers of other cladding materials.

Extending its by now familiar concept of providing a service to architects and designers, Ibstock now established a computer-aided design facility in London. The so-called CAD unit fulfilled two functions; it was on hand to help the group's own research and development and marketing efforts while it was also available to help customers with structural design problems and with the design of individual brick details.

Towards the end of the year, in which the fibres division would push up its profits by 75 per cent on 1985, Ibstock decided to consolidate its dominant management role in Eucalyptus Pulp Mills, the Bahamas-based holding company for the Portuguese wood pulp business.

The company was already effectively running the operation, where Hyde-Thomson was chairman, and the logical conclusion was to raise Ibstock's interest in a business which was proving highly successful.

The Ibstock shareholding was raised from 22.7 per cent to 42.6 per cent. The deal, costing £6.75m and financed by cash and a vendor placing of Ibstock shares, was stimulated by Portugal's entry into the Common Market and the belief among the directors that the country's economic and political outlook now looked increasingly stable.

The share purchase, which involved a reduction in the stakes held by two other partners in the Eucalyptus Pulp business, had to win special clearance from the Takeover Panel in the City because of the transfer of shares between owners and because Eucalyptus Pulp was a non-resident company.

The transaction was completed early in 1987, shortly before Eucalyptus Pulp raised finance for expansion into other fields by reducing its own stake in Caima from over 93 per cent to 76 per cent. Ibstock's interests in forest products would be further significantly advanced later in the same year.

In 1986 there had been further heavy investment, with more than £6m earmarked for UK projects, much of it channelled into improving production processes at a number of plants across the country.

An inevitable casualty was group debt and, by the summer, Ian Maclellan was acknowledging that, for a capital-intensive business operating in a highly cyclical industry, Ibstock was borrowing too heavily.

With total investment within the group set to reach as much as £10m during 1986, capital expenditure over the latest three-year period would total about £37m - a level vastly in excess of depreciation and internal resources.

The answer lay in a rights issue to tidy up the balance sheet. In June the directors announced they would be asking shareholders for £23m via a one-for-four issue in order to help cut borrowings. Without it the group calculated that net debt at the year-end would have risen to around £35m, against shareholders' funds of £65m.

There were critics who suggested that the issue - priced at 148p - would have been better timed earlier on, when its share price had been pushing £2. Even so, the equity base of the business had been strengthened, leaving it well placed to expand further.

Ibstock left 1986 from another solid launching pad with group pre-tax profits rising to £18.5m on turnover of £130m.

14

A new broom

THE next 12 months were to bring excellent financial results throughout the business but high drama within the top rank of Ibstock's management.

It was time for a sea-change in the group's development. There was a growing awareness that Ibstock had become too dependent on one market and that it now needed to broaden its product base. As the last-surviving significant independent brickmaker, nothing less would secure its future. If it failed to act, it would get gobbled up.

After years of attempting to shoulder a range of responsibilities which were now too much for one man, Hyde-Thomson finally decided that, if the business was to rise to the challenge, the time had arrived to shed his executive functions. Though he would remain chairman, someone else would be required to take responsibility for the day-to-day running of the business.

It was the source of some criticism, both within the group and beyond, that by the time the need for a change had become pressing, the chairman had not lined up any obvious successor to take over the helm.

Candidates within the company were few, principally

limited to Richard Boxall, who was busy rebuilding the US operations, and Ian Maclellan, the astute finance director who, after eight years with the group, was still very much a new boy and only 39.

The chairman, however, decided to seek a solution outside. He found Peter Woodman, the 46-year chief executive of Tarmac's building and industrial products division - itself a bigger business than Ibstock - who 10 years previously had become the group's youngest-ever main board director.

Woodman did not know Hyde-Thomson, though the name Ibstock Johnsen was very familiar. He made his own inquiries, some of them through Philip Ling, an occasional acquaintance with whom he had once gone skiing and who encouraged him to pursue the opportunity of a lifetime. Woodman was a solicitor by profession whose career in the building and civil engineering sector had gained him a reputation as a high-flier. His energy and enthusiasm, coupled with sound experience of the building materials sector accumulated in one of the country's most consistently successful businesses, made him an exciting choice.

He took up his new post as group managing director of Ibstock in March and the business prepared for what promised to be a fresh and challenging period of development. His role, as he put it, was to drive the group forward and to seize the right opportunities to expand the business in the interests of employees and shareholders.

Woodman recalls: "I was very attracted to the idea of running what everyone knew was a quality business. It had a solid base from which to diversify, though it was understood we were not going to stray beyond the building materials sector.

"My first impressions were of an excellent company run by a man regarded as a somewhat aloof but honourable patrician with a knowledge of brick which was second to none."

He could hardly have arrived at a more buoyant time. In the UK a lively market, strong prices and further success in containing costs meant there were further improvements in profitability. There was more new investment to improve the product mix, with additional increases in capacity established at Himley, Roughdales and at Leicester, where production of aesthetically attractive, soft mud bricks and special shapes was being stepped up. Demand for clay roof tiles was also particularly encouraging.

There were also changes within the division's

management. Graham Walker recruited Robin Robertson as divisional finance director while Malcolm Peatfield was enlisted as head of marketing and business planning.

After 12 years with the company and having excelled in running the flagship Leicester plant, Martyn Clamp joined the building products board as director in charge of the northern region. His arrival coincided with the departure from the board as a non-executive director, after 52 years service to the brick industry which he loved, of David Jones.

In the US the strategy to raise penetration in the commercial and industrial construction markets was paying off, thereby lessening the dependence on a housing sector which had previously led to such perilous trading conditions. All plants were working to capacity and the level of despatches also broke new ground.

The business was already being helped by a resurgence in the use of brick and, given the new popularity for moulded lines, their production at the Mid-Atlantic plant in Pennsylvania was raised as output of wire-cut bricks was reduced.

The Hanley plant acquisition had quickly begun to justify itself and Glen-Gery was increasingly optimistic of building a national market for the architectural facing bricks being produced by the Pittsburgh factory. Glen-Gery would take about six per cent of a US market set to soak up seven billion bricks before the year was out. At that level its share of the American market was only slightly lower than that being enjoyed in the UK.

There would also be further important diversifications during 1987. Towards the year-end Glen-Gery moved to develop its range of clay paver products by buying the assets of the Capital Concrete Pipe Company of Laurel, Maryland. The business, which was not particularly successful at the time of acquisition, provided the business with a concrete paving facility as well as a pipe-making operation. It represented a strategic step in the regional paving market which also broadened the range of concrete products.

The pattern of success was being repeated in the fibres - now re-christened forest products - division. The year had already got off to a confident start with the decision in January to raise Ibstock's investment in Eucalyptus Pulp Mills and, in turn, management and equity control of the Caima pulp mill operation.

It was to be a record year for the division, with demand for eucalyptus wood pulp remaining firm and significant price increases helping Caima's profitability. By the mid-year mark its profits would exceed those for the whole of the previous year.

As 1987 drew to a close the division took two steps which were to transform its role from that of a useful but junior subsidiary operation into a major contributor of group profits. They would also help change the profile of the group. Having already raised its stake in Eucalyptus a newly-led Ibstock dug deeper into its pocket to mount a full bid for the remaining shares which it did not own in the Portuguese business.

In the opinion of Maclellan and Woodman the existing situation had simply not made any sense. Ibstock owned a stake in Caima, which it had gradually raised, but there was no strategy behind it and, given the size of its interest, the group had no real say in its management. According to Woodman: "It was a case of either winning control or of getting out. Paul, as usual, played a very effective devil's advocate but was also in favour."

Together with the earlier purchase of Eucalyptus shares the group paid out nearly £68m in shares and cash. The deal, in turn, gave Ibstock 76 per cent of Caima, by now one of Portugal's largest publicly-quoted companies with a good management team and ambitious plans for diversification.

As the offer went unconditional the development of the group's forest product interests took a spectacular stride forward. In the sort of decision which might well never have been taken before the arrival of Peter Woodman, Ibstock decided to expand its pulp and timber agency operations, as represented by Johnsen, Jorgensen and Wettre, by making a play in December for the Price & Pierce group, one of the world's oldest timber products agencies.

Price & Pierce were the biggest timber agents in the UK, with major interests in North America and the Far East and responsiblity for handling huge volumes of timber exported from the Soviet Union.

The business had a fine reputation but its financial performance had been in decline. It had been acquired by Tozer Kemsley & Millbourn Holdings, the international trading group, which had subsequently sold on the business to a commodity trading subsidiary of Sears Roebuck, the huge Chicago-based US stores group.

The commodities venture had gone awry, piling up heavy

losses and, in turn, forcing Sears to divest itself of the Price & Pierce operation. It had offered a management buyout, without success, and decided to put the business on the market. In 1987 it had managed to record pre-tax profits of just over £1m on a turnover magnified by its own product sales, as well as those recorded on an agency basis for principals, of well over £100m.

The company's availability drew considerable interest from potential purchasers as the management, headed by chief executive Christopher Allanson, let it be known that they would prefer to end up in British hands and under the control of an owner who knew the pulp and timber business.

Richard Johnsen kept very close to the situation as it developed and he played an important role in ensuring a successful acquisition for Ibstock. "Sears knew we were a good company and the people at Price & Pierce felt comfortable with us. We beat all other suitors and, for £5.6m, the deal proved very good value for money."

A rationalisation programme was immediately put into effect, with staff worldwide reduced from well over 500 to nearer 200. Tighter management and financial disciplines were introduced and unprofitable parts of the business were quickly identified for disposal or closure.

Although the purchase came too late to affect group performance for 1987, it would have a dramatic impact the following year. Even so Woodman was able to tell shareholders: "We now have a wealth of knowledge and expertise in world-wide timber markets both from a manufacturing and agency services point of view. The forest products division has an important role to play in the future development of the group."

The report and accounts for 1987 read like a dream. Pre-tax profits had risen by no less than 93 per cent on top of the near two-thirds improvement of the previous year. Return on capital rose to 28 per cent while return on sales reached 25 per cent. In a cash-rich year an opening net debt figure of £7m was converted to a closing net cash figure of £28m.

As for bricks, Ibstock Johnsen plants in Britain, the US and Belgium had sold 806 million bricks of which 58 per cent had gone to US customers.

In the annual report for 1987 Woodman said that, in his short time with the company, he had got to know the group's senior managers and he was satisfied that he had an able, skilled and enthusiastic team working throughout the business.

Like him, they were committed to building its strengths and to developing the existing group with a blend of organic growth and acquisition. In private, however, there were some worrying undercurrents swirling around the boardroom.

Having stepped back from day-to-day running of the company, something he did not find particularly easy, Hyde-Thomson let his new man make the running.

Most of Woodman's colleagues quickly appreciated his undoubted attributes as a businessman, though some had never been likely to give a ringing endorsement to someone who was, after all, an outsider. As Ian Maclellan put it: "Some people were more prepared to give the new man a chance than others. Some had made up their minds about him even before he arrived."

Woodman was only too well aware from the outset that he had a big job on his hands to prove he was worthy of the responsibility. But if the new broom's business skills were not in doubt, it was not long before his management style began to look increasingly out of step in a group well used to a considered, deliberative approach to decision-making. A clash of management styles began to emerge.

Some of Woodman's senior colleagues pointed to the Tarmac approach to management, on which Woodman had been raised. There, they claimed, major decisions were made in committee, eventually to be rubber-stamped by the directors.

At Ibstock things were different, with decisions being mulled over by the directors in detail, admittedly for too long on some occasions. To Woodman the Ibstock board looked like a time-wasting talking shop in which everyone said their piece and decisions were often put back.

Colleagues also became increasingly uneasy about what they saw as a "divide and rule" element about his management approach. For a team which was used to pulling together, the style was an unwelcome one.

But Woodman was the boss and determined to manage his way, an approach which began to raise hackles. In an attempt to establish close working relationships with his colleagues he set up a group executive committee charged with preparing plans to put to the board. There were new more formalised business systems to replace some of the old ad-hoc unwritten arrangements which had gone before.

If the new chief executive's activities were a source of growing unease within the upper echelons of the business,

Ibstock itself showed all the outward signs of confidence and mounting success as it entered 1988.

The first month of the year brought another acquisition in Portugal, this time of Pinto Basto Comercial, a port handling, freight forwarding and courier services operation. At a cost of just over £5m the business was brought in under an expanding Caima umbrella.

At home, where brick sales were on their way to another record and a fresh wave of capital investment projects were underway, Ibstock trained its eyes on one of the country's oldest family-owned brick manufacturers.

Wakefield-based George Armitage & Sons had been founded in 1824 and was now run by Geoffrey Armitage, the great-great grandson of the founder and a man well-known to Ibstock's own chairman.

The business operated two brick plants in west Yorkshire and one in Lancashire. Employing around 400 people Armitage accounted for around 2.5 per cent of British brick sales but held around 16 per cent of the engineering brick market. Total output was running at around 110 million bricks a year.

In October 1987 the company had openly put itself on the market when the chairman announced that the number of family shareholders had risen over the years to well over 100 and that some, who wanted to realise their shareholdings, were frustrated by its unlisted status. Armitage, he said, had decided the business would be better off as part of a larger group which would provide it with an opportunity to expand. It would also make it less vulnerable to the aggressive pricing and marketing policies of larger rivals.

Armitage sent a prospectus to a number of potential buyers and said it would draw up a shortlist and ask for preliminary offers. The response was immediate with around one dozen companies declaring an interest in taking over one of the few remaining independent brick manufacturers.

Ibstock considered making its own bid but, with 1988 only eight days old, Armitage announced that it had agreed a £69m deal with Hanson, the most obvious suitor of them all. The purchase would be done through Butterley Brick and the board, which controlled 20 per cent of the stock, would be recommending it to shareholders.

Mr. Anthony Cotton, chairman of Butterley, revealing the deal, expressed confidence that the agreement would not raise any problems with the Office of Fair Trading given that the marriage would only give the newly-enlarged business about 20 per cent of the engineering brick market.

His view was echoed by Geoffrey Armitage, who said he did not believe there was much of a chance of the OFT taking an interest in the proposed get-together. Both men were wrong.

Less than a month later, the Department of Trade and Industry, having received a report from the OFT, announced that the bid was to be referred to the Monopolies and Mergers Commission for investigation. The offer, it said, raised competition issues for the supply of engineering bricks in England and Wales and for some kinds of facing bricks in the north and the Midlands. The decision was both surprising and disappointing for Armitage which, days later, was to reveal a near-doubling of profits to just under £6m.

Two weeks passed and Hanson announced that, at the request of Armitage, it was abandoning its attempt to win control of the business. It would have been happy to go through the reference, it added, but Armitage was anxious to get on and find another buyer prepared to make a bid of a similar magnitude.

At Ibstock the possibility of winning the prize which appeared to have escaped its grasp was revived. Woodman said the company remained extremely interested in acquiring Armitage, although he feared he could again be outbid in the face of strong competition.

Even so Ibstock and Armitage sat down to talk while the companies' financial advisers jointly approached the Department of Trade and Industry to establish whether any new bid would encounter the same obstacles as the abortive Hanson approach.

By the end of April Lord Young, the Trade and Industry Secretary, took the unusual step of clearing a possible bid for Armitage from Ibstock. Armitage said the decision did not mean takeover terms with Ibstock had been agreed and that it was continuing to talk to other interested parties. Talk it did and while Ibstock contemplated a deal, it was pipped to the takeover post.

Marshalls Halifax, the Yorkshire concrete products company, brought to an end the long-running saga by quickly negotiating a £70m purchase package for the Armitage business, a higher figure by about £5m than Ibstock had been contemplating. It had lost the battle and Woodman declared that it would not have been in the interests of his shareholders to have made a better offer.

The deal concluded a hectic period of takeover activity among small and medium-sized brick makers, during which time names like Severn Valley, Nottingham Brick, Ockley Brick and Hawkins Tiles had been snapped up by big names which included Tarmac, Blue Circle and Marley. By now only Ibstock, Baggeridge Brick and Blockleys remained as independently-quoted brickmakers.

If Ibstock had let slip from its grasp another useful acquisition, it almost at once proceeded to make amends on the other side of the Atlantic where it purchased for £8.8m the business of New Jersey Shale, the only brickmaking operation in the State, which sat on the edge of the greater New York market. It would enable Glen-Gery to provide a better service to the New York and New Jersey markets.

The takeover was modest by comparison with some of Ibstock's recent deals but Woodman was by now also frying much bigger fish. After his arrival the group managing director had concluded that the domestic business had, to some extent, been neglected. Having built up its pre-eminent position within its own sector, he believed it had dragged its feet on improving efficiency and in reducing costs. "A lot had to be done at home before thinking about other, more glamorous things," he would say later.

Despite his reputation as a fast mover he had, if anything, detected some impatience among his colleagues that progress towards broadening the group's product base had been slow. "They wanted to see the big deal and time was moving on."

While a couple of opportunities for acquiring UK companies which would have fitted neatly into the business were considered, they had not materialised. One was Aberdeen Construction, which was about to be broken up and which offered rich pickings in any asset-stripping exercise. Ibstock could have emerged from a deal with a concrete block and natural stone business which would have fitted in well. It was not, however, Ibstock's style.

An opportunity for a major acquisition of a brick and stone business in the US had also emerged and was being enthusiastically backed by Boxall. It was an attractive opportunity and Ibstock had built up an equity stake in the operation. The would-be target was not, however, prepared to talk and Ibstock was not interested in a hostile bid.

But with the deal on the back-burner another major takeover opportunity arose. It would test the nerve of the most ambitious management team - and would have an unfortunate and unhappy ending.

15

The wrong chemistry

THE group chief executive had meant what he said when he told shareholders that he intended to drive the business forward. Where better than to fulfil corporate aspirations for further expansion and climbing profits than the US?

With the Glen-Gery operation now, after years of struggle, on a sound and confident footing, another major move in the US as part of the group's overall acquisition programme seemed entirely sensible.

Another suitable, very large target had, by now, been located. It was a Nashville, Tennessee, manufacturer of vinyl cladding and windows, now being run by a former Ibstock employee in the US. The view, shared by most of the other directors, was that it would neatly complement the US business and provide the group with a separate source of income and profits. It would, however, cost more than $200m.

Though there had been, from the outset, some natural doubts among Woodman's colleagues over the scale of the proposal, the plan had been actively pursued by Ibstock's top team. A great deal of time and money went into the necessary appraisal of the US business, which had been the subject of a management buyout funded by General Electric. But as the exercise progressed some of the original misgivings in the boardroom over the deal began to grow amongst Woodman's colleagues, who were increasingly alarmed by a deterioration in the financial performance of their takeover target. As an agreed deal reached its final stages attitudes began to change within Ibstock; there were too many uncertainties, too big a downside if everything went wrong, far too much at stake for a group which had just spent the last few years struggling back from losses to achieve record profits.

Woodman shared the reservations but was determined to see whether Ibstock could capitalise on the situation by going back to the negotiating table and extracting a better deal. "I wanted a mandate from the board to return and have another go and then to report back. I could not possibly have recommended it on the terms we had originally agreed. But I wanted one, final try."

So close was the completion of the acquisition that there were fears about the legal consequences of pulling out at such a late stage. Even so, to some directors the prospect of a law suit looked preferable to buying a business arguably about to take a nose dive.

By now support for the takeover had entirely collapsed and Woodman realised he was isolated. He told the chairman he would need a mandate from his colleagues or he would have to go.

The focus moved to Hyde-Thomson, who saw his managing director out on a limb but who also found himself effectively on the receiving end of an ultimatum from some of the other directors; either Woodman would have to go or Ibstock faced losing some of its key personnel.

The choice was his but it was a choice he had to make without delay. According to Michael Keeling: "From the beginning I had regarded the purchase as extremely risky. There was an enormous goodwill element attached to it and the cash and shares deals would effectively have wiped out the shareholders' interest in the balance sheet.

"On top of everything else, the performance of the business in question had started to deteriorate. Peter Woodman wanted to try and renegotiate but the rest of us were opposed to going on. The whole thing had got entirely out of hand and, right up until the very end, it was not clear Paul was going to agree with us that the chief executive had to go."

In the event the chairman decisively backed the

remainder of his board. The man who had been appointed only 16 months before to steer Ibstock through the next phase of its development resigned during the first week in July 1988.

Woodman was bitterly disappointed. He had established no power base within the company, which he believed had again demonstrated an innate conservatism that threatened to undermine its ambitious expansion plans.

The newspaper headlines provided the sort of publicity that Ibstock would have preferred to avoid, claiming its chief executive had gone following a serious policy rift. There was plenty of inspired guesswork about the specific reasons for the abrupt departure of a man who had been seen from outside as the new driving force behind the business.

There were claims that he had gone because no-one shared his view about the need for further acquisitions and that, in future, any growth would be organic and not dependent upon continuing takeovers.

The chairman, though providing no hint of the huge deal which had collapsed, offered the following explanation to the newspapers: "It was more a question of style than strategy and the City should not take from this that the board is lilly-livered when it comes to acquisitions."

He added: "Sometimes the chemistry between individuals is not right and, in the end, I had to tell him that it was just not working out."

Woodman told City journalists that he was very disappointed to be leaving. He explained: "There was a fundamental difference over where the company should go and it came to a head in the past couple of months."

The verdicts within Ibstock on the episode and on Woodman himself were fairly uniform. According to Maclellan: "He muffed a great opportunity. It was a once-in-a-lifetime chance but he managed to end up alienating the people whose support he needed."

Maclellan was not alone in believing that things might have been different if Woodman's undoubted business acumen had been twinned with a less strident approach to his colleagues: "The company's misjudgment lay in not choosing someone with just sufficient charm to win people over. We needed someone to win our hearts as well as our minds and Peter failed to do it."

Michael Chamberlain was not surprised at the outcome. "He was a bundle of energy and enthusiasm and was wildly ambitious for himself and for the business. But he forgot to take everyone else with him."

Peter Johnsen thought extremely highly of Woodman but agreed his executive style did not fit. "His approach to decision-making simply did not work alongside ours. He had excellent ambitions for the business but failed to take account of our own, special culture."

The same conclusion was reached by Richard Johnsen. "The great problem was that he wanted to go too fast and too much on his own. We had been used to a different pace and always moved in agreement. I suppose he felt we were much too set in our ways and too conservative.

"Tarmac's approach to business was a world away from ours. He should have taken account of that and acted accordingly. He had fine business credentials but was the wrong man for us. It was a collective mistake."

According to Woodman: "It could not have gone on much longer without an explosion. It would never have worked so it was good that it ended when it did. It is all over now but I wish them luck."

Woodman's departure left the chairman to fill the breach. The solution was to make Maclellan and Boxall joint managing directors. Their skills were beyond question and there was an immediate need to close ranks and to limit any damage inflicted upon a company not used to internal traumas.

Boxall, now 52, had always been the brick enthusiast; a man who had been taught by his own father, a London Brick research and development engineer, that brickmaking was a science not an art.

His fascination with the challenges of mass production and of quality control had been compelling enough to wean him away from a career in the navy and into the clay industry. His interest had not waned over the intervening years.

More than 10 years his junior, Maclellan had no such background, no such commitment to brick. Like his father, he had trained as an accountant and had found himself working in the commercial property sector during the dark days of the early 1970s.

After a spell as treasurer at Lonrho, the international conglomerate headed by Mr. "Tiny" Rowland, he had gone to Ibstock which was small enough to give him real responsibility and ambitious enough to offer interesting personal prospects.

Though Maclellan was, first of all, a financier, for whom brick is the vehicle for creating profits, he readily acknowledges the grip it has on others. Among all his colleagues, he would have least qualms about changing the core business of Ibstock if that became necessary to ensure its future success.

There were those who believe that the decision to have joint executives, borne out of necessity at the time, is not necessarily the ideal solution. But there are sufficient examples of major businesses being jointly run to demonstrate that the principle is workable. The arrangement, however, remains an undeniable source of unease in the City and a reminder that the question of Hyde-Thomson's succession has not been concluded by the end of the 1980s.

Closing ranks after Woodman's departure meant getting on with business. His sudden exit had at once led to a flurry of speculation to the effect that Ibstock now appeared vulnerable and that it could again soon find itself on the receiving end of another unwelcome bid.

At the end of July the group put the seal on another acquisition in Portugal, acquiring for £6.4m an 80 per cent stake in Fabrica Ceramica de Valadares, one of the country's leading manufacturers of ceramic sanitaryware.

The deal was concluded through Caima and at once gave the group 30 per cent of the domestic market, enabling the local business to diversify away from the highly cyclical forest products operation. Valadares, situated near Oporto, which had been founded in 1921, employed more than 500 people and had net assets of just under £10m. About 45 per cent of total sales, running at around £10m a year, went to export markets, mainly to the UK, the US and to France.

Neither had the group done with acquisitions in its other overseas stronghold. Following on from the summer purchase of New Jersey Shale, Glen-Gery was by the end of 1988 ready to extend further market area and product range with the £10.5m purchase of Midland Brick.

The business had two plants in Iowa and one in Missouri providing a combined annual capacity of 100 million bricks, as well as sales offices, showrooms and distribution centres around its market area.

The purchase extended Glen-Gery's primary market to the west. Coupled with the commissioning of the Iberia plant in Ohio, initially capable of producing up to 50m moulded and extruded bricks, it enabled the business to strengthen its grip on the mid-west as it had done in the north east. The move demonstrated its determination not to be hemmed in and to be able to move its products between the two areas upon which its activities were now firmly based.

The acquisition was quickly followed by the purchase for £1.6m of Gomoljak, a concrete block and masonry distribution business at Annapolis, Maryland. In the UK Ibstock said that it was unlikely to acquire more brick manufacturers in the US unless a special opportunity arose. It was, however, interested in expanding its concrete products operation to meet growing demand in the US, a market considered to be behind the UK in the use of concrete block paving.

The strategy would soon be pursued again with the acquisition of the Kerr Concrete Pipe Company and its Cayuga Pipe subsidiary. The business operated a plant in southern New Jersey and one near Philadelphia, producing a range of concrete pipe and fittings for storm and surface water drainage.

The deal, in early 1989, brought the tally of US concrete pipe plants and block plants to three of each. Glen-Gery now had a sizeable concrete products business in the north-east, well-placed for the manufacture and sale of interlocking concrete paving and other concrete building products.

As in so many previous years Ibstock Johnsen ended 1988 on a buoyant note. When the final results became known they showed pre-tax profits had jumped 57 per cent to £56.3m, nine times those of 1983. Group turnover had leaped from £145m to £368m, much of the increase stemming from newly-expanded Portuguese operations.

In a year which had seen £51m spent on acquisitions and a record £24m on new capital equipment, earnings per share were up 22 per cent to just under 19p, a figure which brought particular satisfaction to Ian Maclellan. He could proudly point to a growth performance in earnings that, over the previous few years, had put Ibstock Johnsen second only to Lucas, the motor components group which had been undergoing a long-awaited recovery.

For those wanting a larger stake in the Ibstock success story shareholders would also be able to receive their dividends as shares, rather than cash.

In the UK, where profits rose by 28 per cent to nearly £30m, brick sales reached another record, with all production units working at full capacity and stocks lying at historically low levels.

As in almost every other year capital investment had proceeded apace, the end products for 1988 including the new tunnel kiln at Leicester and major improvements to production facilities at Cattybrook. There were more new products, like the "Manor" range from Roughdales and the "Classic" from Himley, which would soon find themselves on display alongside the group's other lines at its new brickwork design centre at Albany House next to Regent's Park in London.

In America profits moved ahead as the market for bricks and building materials weakened and prices softened in the face of declining housebuilding activity. Glen-Gery's strenuous efforts to reduce its dependability on the housing sector was paying off.

Within the increasingly important forest products division, both Caima and Price & Pierce had lived up to expectations in developing a third significant arm to group operations. Following the Pinto Basto and Valadares purchases, Caima had been transformed from a pulp company to a holding company with four divisions, each with its own Portuguese chief executive.

Lutterworth House, group headquarters in Leicestershire.

The year-end also brought the retirement of Peter Johnsen, a director of Ibstock Johnsen since the two companies joined forces in 1970. Mr. Colin Hope, the 55-year old group managing director of T & N - previously known as Turner & Newall - joined the board as a non-executive director to share with Ibstock the benefit of his wide industrial and corporate experience. In early 1989 Roger List, the company secretary for 23 years and, in the words of the chairman, "a first-rate counsellor and friend to the board," also took his leave of the company on retirement.

In his annual statement for the year Hyde-Thomson paid tribute to Ibstock's workforce, which had been asked for a great deal and which, yet again, had duly delivered. With more difficult trading conditions on the international horizon in 1989 they would be expected to do no less in the following 12 months - and in the years to come.

The Ibstock board in 1989. From left to right Colin Hope, Richard Boxall, Paul Hyde-Thomson, Philip Ling, Ian Maclellan, Graham Walker and Michael Keeling.

16

The way ahead

AS Ibstock Johnsen prepares for the last decade of the 20th Century the group whose operations now stretch from the Ardennes to the heart of the American mid-west has little in common with the business started a few miles from Leicester more than 160 years earlier. Only a part of its name and its continuing presence on the same site provide a clue to its origins and a starting point for any investigation of its history.

Ibstock has prospered for the most straightforward of commercial reasons. It has well understood its product and its market place, it has tried to shape demand, rather than merely respond to it, and it has always endeavoured, via a commercial ethic based on quality and customer care, to produce the best.

The business has also had the additional advantage of being passed, successively, through the hands of five members of the same family. A lineage of rich experience has provided a continuity of style and management which, despite some continuing misgivings over aspects of its approach, has proved consistently successful.

Ibstock has always been ultimately in the hands of people with a special affection for brick, none more so than Paul Hyde-Thomson whose high personal reputation has persisted over the years and has spread throughout the industry. Giants like Hanson readily sing the praises of a man whom they describe as both a pioneer and an elder statesman in a sector which has extended to him its fullest respects. The chairman of Ibstock draws the same observations from those who have worked closely with him. According to Tony King: "He took a fairly ordinary family business and turned it into a large, highly respected and successful leader in its field. His apparently conventional attitude often conceals a highly unconventional approach to business, which has paid off time and time again." In the words of Tony Cadman: "He is a great diplomat and a highly impressive advocate for his business and for the industry. He is never impolite but possesses a stonewalling technique which is second-to-none.

"Always quiet and thoughtful, he contains his forcefulness behind a gentle exterior. His contribution to the development of the entire industry has been a decisive one."

More succinctly, Graham Walker says: "I can imagine my own life without Ibstock but what on earth will Ibstock be like without Paul Hyde-Thomson?"

Ibstock's chairman - still called "Mr. Paul" by some of the old-timers at the Ibstock works - would accept that he may not readily put people at ease. He has been called "sphinx-like" and remote and his ability to remain unruffled in distinctly unsettling circumstances has raised the blood pressure of more than a few of his colleagues. He has sometimes made the wrong decisions; it would be unique if the man at the helm of a company for so many years had not done so.

Some attempts at expansion, most notably overseas, have failed but there has always been a readiness within the group to take the initiative, thanks to the security provided by its core business at home.

As one close colleague says of him: "Not all his attempts to broaden the business have succeeded. But although we might have stumbled, he has always been free to have another shot because everyone knows where the bread and butter is coming from."

One of Ibstock's biggest problems in seeking to diversify has been the extraordinary success of its principal operation. Ian Maclellan explains: "Nearly every time we have looked to see how we could broaden the base of the group, we have had to compare the possible margins achievable with those we can consistently win on making brick. In the UK, our margins beat those on almost any other product, apart from some high-technology innovations."

With surplus cashflow pumped into buying and building brick-making capacity, Ibstock has continually refined the business of production and the search for maximum profitability. Even so some competitors believe that the group's position as the number one marketing practitioner has not yet been repeated in terms of its production expertise.

It is not a view widely shared within the business. According to Maclellan: "We have been so damned successful at what we do best that, almost every time someone says let's have a go at something else, we take one look at our 30 per cent margins and sit tight."

But, like every other business, Ibstock is having to keep abreast of new production innovations which bring with them fresh challenges of their own. Naturally enough Ibstock remains wary of implementing changes which threaten to destroy the appealing variety of product which provides the key to its success. The challenge is to reduce costs without spoiling an all-important flexibility.

As Jack Watton, the Himley manager, puts it: "Some of our most interesting colours and finishes are because of so-called "inefficient" kilns. Modern plant can produce very monotone, boring bricks. You have to be wary of computerisation when you want something different."

The chairman openly acknowledges that strategic errors have been made during the development of the business, not least in approaching fundamentally different overseas markets as though they were no more than an extension of Ibstock's domestic business, of sometimes being too cautious in contemplating acquisitions and sometimes failing to invest sufficiently in some of its production plant.

They are the sort of admissions, coupled with the insistence of his business partners that any misjudgments have almost always been collective ones, which provide a further measure of Hyde-Thomson's own approach to business and of the allegiance which he inspires in others.

He is also held to account for a reserve which makes it difficult for him to hand out the sort of back-slapping compliment which entails little effort but which can work wonders for morale.

All reservations are minor ones. Michael Keeling sums up the man who essentially made Ibstock what it is: "He has an almost unique understanding of the economics of brickmaking and of how you squeeze every ounce of profitability from them, without compromising the quality of the product. He is quite unlike any other brickmaker."

Perhaps the most often-heard criticism levelled against him is that he has occasionally selected the wrong people for the job and that, having done so, he can be slow to withdraw his loyalty in the face of the evidence. Kindness and friendship have sometimes overruled more hard-headed corporate considerations.

More specifically, his failure to produce a natural successor is seen, by outsiders, as an important weakness which still colours their opinion of the business.

The principal of bringing on management talent should extend down through the business and, in this respect, the group has made significant steps forward.

According to Graham Walker, the process of creating the next generation of top management is already well underway: "We have 30 senior managers running our units. No other company in the business has such a wealth of ability. If I worked for someone else, I would be headhunting them."

In the UK Ibstock has virtually achieved its ambition to be a national brickmaker, offering a range of product to its customers which enables them to make the most imaginative use of brick and to utilise an essentially simple building material to its best advantage. Scotland remains Ibstock-free, save for a design centre. Unhelpful clays and a strong, national preference for rendered housing has kept demand low, though Ibstock plants in the north do supply customers north of the border.

But while the group has established a national sales force, its encouragement of plant-by-plant autonomy has retained a healthy spirit of internal competition which would be absent from a more centrally-oriented business machine.

There can be no let-up, however, even in respect of its supreme marketing skills. The business has always tried to create a supportive and imaginative environment in which its sales force can work.

As for additional capacity, some further modest acquisitions of suitable brick producing businesses can never be discounted, though there are strong arguments for Ibstock building its own new plants.

The primary emphasis, however, will be on investing in existing plant to boost output, improve efficiency and broaden the appeal of a product range which now extends to 150 alternatives, a total which excludes variations in size and which takes no account of Ibstock's readiness to produce custom-made brick lines for particular projects.

By 1988 Ibstock was delivering 330 million bricks - around 10 million of them hand-made - to its UK customers, enabling it to claim about 10 per cent of the national facings market. Of the total UK capacity between four and five per cent was accounted for by specials.

There will be new challenges apart from maintaining and improving the group's market share and efficiently coping with the inevitable economic cycles which inflict themselves upon construction activity.

With protection of the environment daily becoming a more pressing political and commercial priority, the extractive industries in general and groups like Ibstock in particular will also be expected to play a lead role in ensuring that economic success can happily co-exist with a healthy environment.

Graham Walker emphasises: "We can no longer assume that planning permission will always be forthcoming for our activities. People do not want a brickworks on their doorstep and we have to make a far bigger effort to ensure that our activities are compatible with an increasing desire to protect and preserve the environment."

With economic and political ties growing closer within the European Economic Community, it is also encumbent on any commercial enterprise with aspirations for a successful future to prepare for the barrier-free single market of 1992.

Bricks might not be the easiest commodity to transport - despite some well-publicised overseas consignments, Ibstock exports from the UK are minimal - but investment cash travels effortlessly. Every industry faces a future in which their traditional market places are exposed to unparalleled competitive forces.

Ibstock may yet choose to diversify within the UK, further away from the product which it has promoted more successfully than anyone else. The group is not of a size to make a complete break and to buy its way overnight into new activities on a sufficiently large scale to protect it from dependency on its core product.

Yet it may decide to extend further the barriers of its involvement in building products by participating in the manufacture of other widely-used materials. Whatever course it adopts there seems no question that brick will remain at the heart of its domestic operations. Its principal effort will be focused on winning more of the market it knows best.

Further afield Ibstock's international strategy in the run-up to the 1990s appears to offer the most scope for dramatic change.

The corporate profile of Ibstock Johnsen has recently changed fundamentally, with its new emphasis on the forest products activities which historically played a minor role in its affairs and which have served to transmit a confusing image to those observers attempting to put the business into a convenient slot.

The paper and pulp operation, by the end of 1980s, would be contributing around 30 per cent of group profits. The performance effectively challenged the long-standing view of those brick enthusiasts within the group, some of whom barely acknowledged that any other activities existed within Ibstock, that forest products were an uninteresting adjunct to a British and American brick business.

Despite Ibstock's growing exposure to forest products markets, it harbours no aspirations to be a world player in a world commodity market. As with its bricks, the group is happiest performing as a niche player - primarily supplying the quality producers of fine writing and tissue papers - within its chosen industry.

Ibstock may well, however, entertain the idea of linking up with other world players, possibly jointly developing new pulp and paper production facilities or permitting outside investment in its own forest product operations.

Alternatively, or additionally, Ibstock's Portuguese business might begin to acquire other companies, possibly in the building materials field. With one successful ceramic sanitary ware manufacturer under its belt, the way to further acquisitions is already open.

Fresh moves into Europe, from which it retreated after the traumas of the early 1980s, also seem quite likely. Despite some unhappy memories Ibstock appears to have regained its enthusiasm for another sortie across the channel, with the building products sector at the top of the shopping list.

Again the strategy would entail acquisitions or links with foreign companies rather than embarking on start-up situations. The approach will be one of moving in as and when the right opportunities arise.

Paul Hyde-Thomson says the group welcomes the opportunity of expanding within a barrier-free European Community, adding with a suitable touch of sangfroid: "Any lessons learned in the past will not so much put us off as make us wise. We would learn from them and do better the next time round."

The common denominator in any new European initiative would be the chance to capitalise on market-led opportunities. Ibstock, as always, wants to promote and to sell its products on factors other than cost.

In the US Ibstock finds itself with a brick production capacity of more than twice that in the UK. Its plants, by the end of the 1980s, were capable of manufacturing 700 million bricks annually and the business could claim to be among the largest brickmaking operations in the US market. Customers could choose from around 425 different brick types, twice the number in the UK.

But despite Glen-Gery's ultimate success, the business is still regarded suspiciously by some within the group and, more so, by outside observers. The most popular criticism is that bricks in the US never have and never will offer the type of margins to which Ibstock has become accustomed in the UK; it is a fair observation but Ibstock would hardly have extended its business at all if UK-type margins were an essential pre-requisite to any new initiatives. In any case, margins in the UK are unlikely to remain at the levels enjoyed for a period in the latter part of the 20th Century. From outside, the Glen-Gery business, which has been resolutely pulled together after its early traumas, is still seen as a potential achilles heel, vulnerable to the huge swings in demand which characterise the American construction cycle. One competitor reckons that Ibstock has not really decided how to develop its US business. A senior Ibstock director admits that some people in the company would shed few tears if the business were to be disposed of.

Whatever the view the American contribution to group profits - running at around 20 per cent at the end of the 1980s - can no longer be sneezed at. Return on capital employed is also high by US standards.

There are, consequently, no apologies for making the move. According to Ian Maclellan: "If Ibstock had just stayed in brick in the UK it would, by now, have been a subsidiary of another group. We have always wanted to look after our own business, so we had to broaden it. A business has to develop and expand. We had to go forward."

Richard Boxall accepts that there is still a great deal to be done in a market which will never behave like the one on which Ibstock has based its business. "Brick is not the major building material it is in the UK, although the market is so much bigger. It is merely an option and in our market areas many specifiers will be quite likely to use something else. We see that not as a problem but as a real opportunity.

"Margins are not as good because of the intense competition. Our basic strategy, having digested many businesses in a relatively short time, is to make them work better. The performance of our plants varies and our task is to bring up the poor ones to the performance of the very best."

"The alternative is to sell the American operation. But the fact is that we own it and have built it into a healthy business. We are probably about the fourth biggest brick producer in the United States." Of the top five brick makers in America, four are already foreign-owned, and between them they account for over half national brick capacity.

In the short-term there may well be a lull in US expansion and acquisition. There will be continued investment, though not necessarily to add to capacity but to replace older, inefficient production facilities and to reduce costs. The emphasis will be on making existing assets perform better.

Boxall is particularly pleased in succeeding in establishing a good balance between housing and non-housing. Glen-Gery is still more dependent on the housing sector than is Ibstock in the UK, with around 60 per cent of sales utilised for homebuilding. In the UK, a little over half of all sales go into housing. But for most US suppliers the housing market invariably accounts for 80 or 90 per cent of their despatches. It is a balance which gives Glen-Gery the sort of strength that will be needed as it heads into the next downturn in US housing activity.

If the future is an uncertain and unpredictable mix of the unexpected, of successes and failures, Paul Hyde-Thomson has no qualms about Ibstock's ability to rise to the challenge.

It is, he is the first to admit, going to be very difficult to stay ahead of the game in an increasingly competitive market place. "We have taken and maintained a lead in our field because we have successfully persuaded the specifier of brick, along with the final customer, to prefer Ibstock. Our sales force is more numerous and more customer-conscious than ever, but there can be no let-up."

Ibstock, he adds, has always made it a point of honour and of corporate pride to be much closer to the market place than its competition. "It has not just been a case of meeting what we thought the market wanted but of trying to get the market to want what we wanted it to want. That is real marketing."

Ibstock Johnsen, a business with roots stretching back to a crude, Leicestershire coal pit, now enjoys the status of an international group with nearly 5,000 employees, a value on the London Stock Exchange of around £250m and the ability to sell over one billion bricks a year.

The chairman is not overawed by the new challenge his business will confront. "The technology of brickmaking, on which we survive, has not really changed since Egyptian times. You dig up some clay, make a brick shape, dry it, burn it - and then try and sell it."

Such simplistic an analysis might understate the case and Ibstock's own achievements. It is not, however, a bad lesson in the basic art of brickmaking from which Ibstock can embark on the next chapter in its history.

INDEX